THE

DEBORAH

ANOINTING

MICHELLE MᶜCLAIN-WALTERS

CHARISMA
HOUSE

Cover design by Lisa Rae McClure
Design Director: Justin Evans

Visit the author's website at www.michellemcclainministries.com.

Library of Congress Cataloging-in-Publication Data:
McClain-Walters, Michelle.
  The Deborah anointing / by Michelle McClain-Walters.
      pages cm
  Includes bibliographical references.
  ISBN 978-1-62998-606-7 (trade paper) -- ISBN 978-1-62998-607-4 (e-book)
  1. Deborah (Biblical judge) I. Title.
  BS580.D4M33 2015
  222'.32092--dc23

                               2015021977

18 19 20 21 22 — 14 13 12 11 10
Printed in the United States of America

CONTENTS

Introduction: Embracing the Call to Be a Woman
of Power and Influence 1

Chapter 1: Times and Seasons of the Call 9

Chapter 2: Deborah: The Judge and Deliverer 19

Chapter 3: Deborah the Mother 28

Chapter 4: Deborah the Worshipping Warrior 36

Chapter 5: Deborah the Honeybee.................... 48

Chapter 6: Deborah the Prophetess 61

Chapter 7: Deborah and Barak 69

Chapter 8: Jael: A Fierce Warrior 76

Chapter 9: Deborah the Preserver 88

Chapter 10: Deborah the Visionary 99

Chapter 11: Anointed With Power, Designed
for Influence 109

Chapter 12: Lappidoth: The Man Who Takes Care
of the Woman Deborah 122

Notes... 129

EMBRACING THE CALL TO BE A WOMAN OF POWER AND INFLUENCE

Village life ceased. It ceased until I, Deborah, arose; I arose like a mother in Israel.

—JUDGES 5:7

VILLAGE LIFE HAD ceased. The conditions in Deborah's society had become deplorable and tragic. The will of her people had been broken by the cruelty and ruthlessness of their Canaanite oppressors. They were suffering the consequences of their own disobedience before God. There was a great vacuum of the presence of God in the land. Life had almost come to a standstill. Thieves invaded and caused roads to be abandoned due to the danger of assaults. Trade and commerce had obviously collapsed, for caravans could not even get through the bands of outlaws scattered up and down trade routes. There were no children playing outside, no neighbors standing in the yards engaged in conversations, no socializing in any fashion much like the streets of my own Chicago, and maybe like your town too. Many are confined to their homes because of violence. What is the answer to these deplorable conditions? I am. You are.

Woman of God, the Lord is extending a great invitation to you to become a part of His story and to effect history. He is calling ordinary women like you into His extraordinary work.

Make no mistake about it: embracing the marvelous calling of

God is not easy or glamorous. There will always be obstacles to overcome and seemingly more attractive ways to live. Yet, God calls us to live as His ambassadors among the nations, spreading His love and making an eternal difference in the lives of those in our sphere of influence.

It's not about God being a part of your story; it's about your being a part of His story. It's not about who is for you or against you; it's about whom you are for. You are not just a woman who has authority; you are also a woman living under authority.

Will I live consumed with who is for me or against me, or will I live consumed with whom I am for? Am I making my mark and fulfilling some humanistic purpose, or is God making His mark through me?

As the Lord begins to direct you to embrace your calling and the stirring in your heart for His destiny and purpose for you, I believe that you will begin to take on a similar divine urgency and sense of responsibility for things greater than yourself. I believe that you will begin to see yourself as a woman of influence, conviction, and power. There is a divinely inspired cry coming out of your spirit, declaring, "Not on my watch!" The passion and righteous indignation of the Lord is arising in the hearts of women to take up the sword of the Spirit to touch heaven through prayer and intercession to bring reformation on the earth.

Just as Deborah had been called to become the spokeswoman for God, telling of divine revelation and strategy that would lead the nation to victory, I see you taking on this same mantle and walking in the anointing of wisdom and revelation to bring solutions. You will take on these characteristics of the Deborah anointing and will speak the right words to awaken men and women in powerful places to advocate and endorse kingdom rule and advancement.

What Is the Deborah Anointing?

"I, Deborah arose" (Judges 5:7). The Hebrew word translated as "arose"[1] in this passage of Scripture is a compound word that describes the position women must take in this time of crisis in the earth. It means:

1. To arise (hostile sense)—Deborahs will confront the powers of darkness with the power of God, liberating thousands of people around the world.

2. To arise, become powerful—Deborahs will be activated in the power gifts of the Spirit—the gifts of faith, healing, and miracles.

3. To arise, come on the scene—Deborahs will be voices for the voiceless.

4. To stand, to maintain oneself—Deborahs will pioneer a movement among women that will empower the next generation to fulfill their destinies in every area of life.

5. To be established, to be confirmed, to stand, to endure, to be fixed, to be valid, to be proven, to be fulfilled, to persist, to be set, to fulfill, to confirm, to ratify, to establish, to impose, to stir oneself up—Deborahs will have a resolve to stand boldly in the call of God. They will not apologize for the anointing and grace they have to lead. These modern-day Deborahs will have resilience and persistence.

Many who carry a Deborah anointing will be blessed with the gift of leadership. They will be women who have developed the character and ability to inspire and disciple the next generation to walk in the fullness of their call. These modern-day Deborahs will have a lifestyle of prayer and worship that will cause a generation to return to their first love, Jesus. A key theme of the Book of Judges is that it exposes the depravity and corruption of the human heart. Time and time again when God's people cried out for Him to save them, He would empower a deliverer to rescue them. But when the deliverer (judge, prophet, or king) died, the people would slip back into their compromising, permissive lifestyle. Their corrupt hearts were exposed; they loved this world with its bright lights, pleasures, possessions, wealth, honor, false worship, and idolatry.

Modern-day Deborahs will be women after God's heart who will lead a generation to stand for God's ways of righteousness in the midst of a wicked and perverse generation. Deborah's office was between Ramah and Bethel. *Ramah* meaning a place of idolatry and *Bethel* being the house of God. The Deborah anointing is a grace the breaks the idolatry in the human heart and causes it, through mentoring, discipling, and training, to be matured and purified.

The motivation of the modern-day Deborah is the mother's heart. The mothering anointing is returning to this land. This facet of the Deborah anointing is the ability to nurture a generation. One of the major causes of rebellion in the youth of our society is rejection and lack of guidance. Modern-day Deborahs will spend time in the presence of the Lord to gain strategies and insight on how to empower this generation with wisdom and counsel.

Deborah was a wife, mother, intercessor, and prophetess. She was also a judge and a national deliverer. This is not a bad résumé for a middle-aged woman living in an oppressive Middle Eastern culture. We are introduced to her story while she is in full manifestation of her calling. I would like to share with you the key factors that will activate a Deborah anointing. You may not possess all of these characteristics, but it is important for you to cultivate each gift for whatever level of manifestation is needed in developing your call and assignment.

Keys to activating the Deborah anointing

+ Strategic intercessor—Develop a listening ear in the presence of the Lord, and pray toward the fulfillment of the plans the Lord shares with you.

+ Judge—Develop a love and compassion for the people to whom you are sent. Deborah had a deep love for the people of Israel, which she demonstrated as she sat under the palm tree patiently mediating disputes and bringing order and justice to the lives of people miserably oppressed by the cruel government.

+ Prophetess—Operate in a heavenly dimension of a spirit of wisdom and revelation. Deborah did this well, and it was almost as if God had supernaturally implanted a divine compass in her, always guiding her to Him.

+ Mother—Deborah's unique, maternal leadership style extended from the common man to the commonwealth. She had a gathering grace that caused men, women, commanders, and rulers to voluntarily enlist in the army of God. Maternal instinct must return to the earth. We need to pray and decree that young women will develop the heart of a mother once again. Older women must teach the younger women. There must be focused prayer and deliverance against hardness of heart among women in the younger generation.

+ Deliverer/military strategist—The Lord literally dropped a clear prophetic word to summon Barak, the Israeli commander, to rally the troops for battle against insurmountable odds. Although we are not always facing natural battles, as modern-day Deborahs we must cultivate a spirit of prophetic prayer that will enable us to pray accurate and strategic prayers that will cause us to know God's spiritual battle plan.

+ Agitator—To stir up or excite public discussion with the goal of producing change, Deborah stirred up Israel's concern about its low spiritual condition. She did more than just prophesy; she aroused a nation from its lethargy and despair. Modern-day Deborahs will do the same through digital media, books, television/radio broadcasts, and various forums to raise public awareness for the issues that matter to God and bring healing and empowerment to His people.

+ Worshipping warrior—Remain in the presence of the Lord through worship, Bible study, and prayer. For Deborah, worship was the source of her strength. She found peace and power in the presence of the Lord.

Hindrances to the Deborah anointing

+ Fear—Women must be bold and courageous. We cannot operate as Deborahs when we fear men in authority or controversy. God is empowering women to break through many barriers and overcome obstacles set up by the devil to derail them from their God-given destinies. Fearless and humble, women will be co-laborers with Him and with men in redeeming and restoring humanity and the earth.

+ Harsh speaking, aggressiveness, cold-heartedness, Jezebel-like nature—*Deborah* means "honeybee." God is raising up women who have the sting of the bee, deadly to the enemy, yet they will speak sweet and compassionate words of wisdom to those who are in need. Modern-day Deborahs will be bold but not brazen like Jezebel.

+ Slumber and ministry burnout—Deborah declares in Judges 5:12: "Awake, awake, Deborah! Awake, awake, and sing a song!" Many times when dealing with oppressed people, there can be a sense of feeling overwhelmed and hopelessness. Those who have a Deborah anointing will have an anointing to encourage themselves in the Lord through worship.

Deborah demonstrates the possibility of what can happen with any woman today who will allow the Spirit of God to fill and form her life for kingdom purposes. Deborah was a woman used by God to voice His judgment and His prophecy and to spark one of the greatest revivals in history. Women are arising and influencing the world in a way they have never done before. We must be prepared and positioned properly.

Awake! Awake! Deborah!

Will you allow the Holy Spirit to shape and mold you into a leader—whatever the level of authority and capacity—who fits into His perfect will? Will you be trained in the art of intercession and activated in the prophetic to hear and release the word of the Lord to your generation? Will you be a willing leader for God today? Whatever your sphere of influence—at your job, in your home, or at church—will you accept the challenge to stand for God's ways and encourage others to do the same? If your answer is yes, make the following declaration, then join me in the pages that follow to learn how you can embrace the call to be a modern-day Deborah on this earth.

Lord, I pray that You will awaken me to the call You have for my life. Remove any bondage of fear from my heart and mind. Let Your wisdom and courage rest upon me. Awaken me from slumber. Let me walk circumspectly in this hour. I loose myself from passivity and apathy. Let me be alert to Your voice. Let me be aware of Your purpose.

I thank You, Lord, that You are an extraordinary God and You will accomplish extraordinary things through me. I release myself from self-imposed limitations. I break every limitation that the enemy has placed upon my life and has kept me from meeting my full potential.

No longer will I be deceived and trapped by the traditions and opinions of men. For I was created for greatness! I was created to be God's glory carrier throughout the earth. I will arise and be radiant with the glory of the Lord. I will be a beaming lighthouse of hope for many who sit in gross darkness.

Lord, give me words of wisdom that will guide and influence many. I will not remain silent! I break every demonic conspiracy designed to keep me silent! I won't let past failures and disappointments keep me silent. I will open my mouth wide, and God, You will fill it.

God, give me ideas, insight, and concepts to bring deliverance to many. You have anointed me to impart grace to those in my sphere of influence. The words that I speak will release life to a hurting generation. I am not in this world by chance. I'm not in this decade by chance. I'm not reading this book by chance. I am a modern-day Deborah! I stir up and activate the Deborah anointing through this prayer and declaration. In the name of Jesus, amen.

Chapter 1

TIMES AND SEASONS OF THE CALL

To everything there is a season, a time for every purpose
under heaven.

—ECCLESIASTES 3:1

OUR FIRST INTRODUCTION to Deborah and her vitae is quite
impressive. Judges 4:4 states that Deborah was a prophetess, the
wife of Lappidoth, and she was performing duties as the judge of
Israel. Have you ever met someone, and after hearing her con-
fidently and effortlessly rattle off all of her accomplishments,
you feel intimidated, inadequate, and insignificant? Or here is
a good one: have you ever received a prophetic word about all
of the wonderful things you're supposed to accomplish for the
Lord, then said within yourself, "They missed it big time with
that prophecy." You may feel that your past and present reality
are so far from the future the prophetic word declares that it is
hard to find the faith to receive as a real possibility. Or maybe
you appreciated the prophecy but wonder how you would find
the time to accomplish it all.

I want you to take a deep breath and repeat Ecclesiastes 3:17
with me, "There is an appropriate time for every matter and
deed." Oh, how I wish someone had exposed me to this concept
when I was in my twenties. Let me explain. I received my first
prophetic word when I was twenty-five about having an anointing
like Deborah to take to the nations. When I researched through
scriptures and discovered who Deborah was and what she accomplished, I almost worried myself into a nervous breakdown.

I had just come out of a painful divorce, had a two-year-old daughter who had been diagnosed as legally blind, and worked a job with the state that kept me traveling sometimes weekly. It was easier to believe that the prophets had missed it than to add another thing to my plate. What I didn't realize was that Deborah was a middle-aged woman who had probably gone through many seasons in her life before she became all that Scripture details.

The call of God is progressive. He will mature you gradually into the fullness of His plan. I truly believe the Lord will mold and shape you for the Deborah anointing by using all of your life experiences. Every hat you may wear and every role you may play will be significant in your expression of the Deborah anointing.

One of my spiritual fathers, Apostle Alvin Green, gave me a piece of advice that I want to pass along to you. He said, "Michelle, the best way to eat an elephant is one bite at a time!" If you're like me and want to accomplish everything that God has for your life, keep reading this book and let's take the metaphoric bite one chapter at a time. Don't get overwhelmed. Keep saying yes to God in your heart.

I've actually come to learn that God wants to use the whole of our lives. One of Deborah's roles was as a wife. I believe the Spirit of God highlighted this aspect of Deborah's makeup because He wanted to make Deborah relatable to many women. Sometimes we can deify Bible characters without realizing they were just humans who said yes to the call of God. Once you say yes, you will be empowered by the Holy Spirit to fulfill your God-given destiny.

The call of God takes time to develop. God moves in cycles, patterns, times, and seasons. The call of God on your life will have times and season of development and patterns designed by God for implementation. When you understand time correctly, you can grasp God and His purpose for your life. Acts 17:26 says that God has determined our appointed times in advance. If you are going to embrace the call to successfully walk in the Deborah anointing, you must learn to discern the times and seasons God has already ordained for your life and properly align your actions with His timetable.

Women Who Understand Time

One of the keys to Deborah successfully fulfilling the call of God on her life was that she had an ability to discern the times and seasons of God. She balanced her responsibilities of being a wife, judge, and prophetess. She wasn't a woman who wasted time watching soap operas or reality TV. There are some scholars who believe Deborah was from the tribe of Issachar. It's important to understand who the tribe of Issachar was and the important role they played in Deborah's life. In 1 Chronicles 12:32 we see that the sons of Issachar had understanding of the times, and they used that understanding to discern what Israel ought to do. Those from the tribe of Issachar understood the times of God; this understanding gave them insight and wisdom in every situation.

If Deborah was from this tribe, she had this characteristic of Issachar, of discerning times and seasons, in her DNA. She synchronized her life and actions with the time clock of heaven. The essence of the Deborah anointing is to understand that God has a calendar and that He has scheduled times for blessings, deliverance, and even war.

There is nothing more important than time. Time is the measure of life. The quality of your life is determined by how effectively you use time. Actually you become what you do with your time. Time is an interruption of eternity. God created time, He placed man in it, but God doesn't live in time. Time was created to measure life and to take man out of eternity because eternity is timeless. Whatever happens in eternity lasts forever. Jesus reveals Himself as the beginning and the end. Totality rests in Him. Our time in life begins in Him and ends in Him. He is the A to Z. Jesus has already walked through our lives. He has something for us to do every day. He fashioned our days before they ever existed. Our times are in His hands. "To everything there is a season, a time for every purpose" (Eccles. 3:1). God has a destiny for each one of His children, but we must learn to move our feet according to the rhythm of His perfect time.

I believe Deborah had many private victories in discerning the times and seasons of God before she was placed on her public platform. Your private victories are when you are routinely taken through a process of testing by God to prepare you for the call. Private victories are made up of small acts of obedience to the voice of God.

Discerning the Spiritual Seasons of the Call

> And let us not be weary in well doing: for in due season we shall reap, if we faint not.
>
> —Galatians 6:9, kjv

We must understand that the God who ordered the seasons of the earth can rightly order the seasons of your life, bringing you to maturity, ripeness, and productivity in His own due season. God has a timetable for you to manifest your calling. He has a due season or appointed time. Just as there are four natural seasons of winter, spring, summer, and fall, there are also four spiritual seasons of winter, spring, summer, and fall. You must learn the seasons so you will be ready to respond and prepare to navigate and capitalize with God for each transition. Not knowing the proper seasons of your calling is like a seeing a woman wearing a fur coat walking on the beach in summer. It's obvious she is not one who accurately discerns the season.

Spiritual winter: a time of death to self

Winter is the season with the shortest days, limited sunlight, and the lowest average temperatures. It characteristically has the coldest weather with snow and ice. Winter is a time for inclement weather when people want to stay inside and hibernate (Matt. 24:20; Mark 13:18; Acts 27:12; 2 Tim. 4:21; Titus 3:12). Winter is a time when you might feel cold and uncomfortable. Any farmer will tell you that winter is not a time to plant but to begin planning what to plant during the next season.

Your spiritual winter can seem like a time of darkness, as if your life is unfruitful, and you may assume your dreams are dying. But during winter there is no fruit bearing. It is a time when God kills everything in your life that will affect the harvest of the next season in your life. Spiritual winter is the most uncomfortable time for many Christians. However, this is a season to redefine and further develop a relationship with the God of your call. This is when God continues to develop your root system in Him. There He will give you directions for planting new crops in spring, which is the next season. Spiritual winter is the time for evaluation, planning, and preparation. It is a time for letting go of anything that will destroy your call. It is also the time to learn the uniqueness of your call.

In this season God will begin to enlighten the eyes of your understanding (Eph. 1:18). He may give you a calling, assignment, dream, or promise, and you may have no understanding of what it is or how it is supposed to function or be accomplished. You may wonder why God chose you for this calling. You may look around at the ability of others and wonder why God did not call them instead of you. During spiritual winter it is normal to feel as if everyone else seems to be better qualified and better equipped. At the same time you are also wondering why you feel so compelled toward a particular area of ministry or service. This dilemma stirs a desire to seek God about the call on your life.

You may feel as if you are having a "wilderness" experience— as if God is not hearing your prayers or speaking to you. I have heard it taught that the wilderness is a place of God's punishment. I believe that the wilderness is where you finally meet God. Hosea 2:14 gives us a different picture of the wilderness:

Therefore, I will allure her, and bring her into the wilderness, and speak tenderly to her.

The wilderness is the place you begin to see yourself in the light of His glory. It's where you encounter God and kill the beast of your soul that would hinder the call of God. The wilderness is the place where you die to self. The inclination is to pray harder or more, but you must remain in the season of rest.

Spiritual winter is a time of reflection and meditation. It is a season of questions and answers between you and the Holy Spirit for the details of your life. It's a time of measurement. As questions begin to arise in your heart, you may ask the Lord:

+ *Who are You, Lord?* The answer to that question also reveals who you are.

+ *What do You want me to do?* The answer to that question is the opening of clarification and direction for His call on your life.

Spiritual spring: a time to embrace the call

Spring marks the transition from winter into summer. According to the Bible spring is the time when kings go off to war. (See 2 Samuel 11:1; 1 Chronicles 20:1.) Maybe this is why Deborah knew it was time for Israel to go to war.

Springtime is also the rainy season. God aided Deborah and Barak by causing torrential rains to fall from the sky, causing Sisera and his men with nine hundred chariots to be stuck in the mud, causing them to be inoperable.

Spring is the time for romance with descriptions of buds and blossoms (Songs 2:11–14; 7:11–13). Spring brings new leaves and blossoms on the trees.

In the spiritual realm spring is the time to plant and carry out the instructions gleaned from your winter experience. You will began to implement the instructions you've gained from spending time with God in the wilderness. Because you've rested and encountered God in the wilderness, you will have fresh, new revelation of God. This newfound revelation will empower you with spiritual and physical energy to break up your fallow ground.

> The expression, "Break up your fallow ground" (Hos. 10:12; Jer. 4:3) means, "Do not sow your seed among thorns", i.e., break off all your evil habits; clear your hearts of weeds, in order that they may be prepared for the seed of righteousness. Land was allowed to lie fallow that it might become more fruitful; but when in this condition, it soon became overgrown with thorns and weeds. The cultivator of the soil was careful to "break up" his fallow ground, i.e., to clear the field of weeds, before sowing seed in it. So says the prophet, "Break off your evil ways, repent of your sins, cease to do evil, and then the good seed of the word will have room to grow and bear fruit."[1]

Ask yourself: In what ways have I been stagnant or neutral about pursuing the purpose of God for my life? What is required of me to change this position of stagnation and neutrality?

In the spring season begin to develop a new confidence in the God of your calling. There is newfound faith in God's ability to accomplish His calling through you. There is new desire to be equipped and trained in the calling. There is a new aligning of your heart for your assignment, a new desire for deliverance to remove anything that would hinder the call. God will send you new connections, mentors, and relationships to help fulfill the call. Desire to discover the full depth of your calling, assignment, or dream.

Spiritual summer: a time of revelation

Summer is the time to water what has been planted during the spring. Summer is the most dangerous season because of the heat (natural and spiritual). Summer is a time of both growth and of stillness; of hard work in the fields and of relaxing in the cool of the day. Summer is a time for both work and play. This is where you learn to balance your natural life and spiritual calling. This is a time of wisdom and revelation. There will even be opportunity to minister in some level of the call and anointing on your life. Everything seems to come to life after a long winter and spring.

In this summer season you come to know and understand some of the depths, requirements, and specifics of the call. The initial fear and anxiety has calmed down, and you will become confident in accepting the call of God. You will say, "For I know whom I have believed, and am persuaded..." (2 Tim. 1:12).

Paul moved from not knowing God to wanting to know God, and then his desire was fulfilled as he began to relate to the God of the call. You will know God in increasing levels of relational intimacy through worship, prayer, and the Word. You will become confident of what God has called you to do—His purpose. You will be persuaded that the God of the call is able to make sure that His calling is fulfilled in your life.

Ask yourself: How am I growing in my relationship with Jesus? How would I describe my level of confidence in my assignment?

Spiritual fall: a time of harvest and fulfillment

Provided you have been diligent during the previous seasons, fall is the time of harvest. Fall is the time when you will see evidence of your hard work. It is a time of harvesting and storing up for the winter. This is the season filled with anticipation. And if we have been obedient in the other seasons, we will reap a harvest in due season (Gal. 6:9).

Autumn is a season of fruition and reaping. It is a season of thanksgiving and celebration of the abundance and goodness of the earth. In this season you are living with the assurance that the instructions assigned to you in the call of God have been fulfilled or carved out to their fullest expression. This assurance produces a desire for a reward. You realize that there is a reward for those who complete God's assignment according to His blueprint for their lives. You will realize that you have fought a good or honorable fight. You will realize that you have finished your course or your assignment. You will also realize that you have kept the faith, or remained in courage and trust in God and His ability to fulfill everything He has declared for your life.

You will submit yourself to the price or sacrificial demands of God's call, and from that posture of humility you will evoke a response from God, receiving your reward.

> But without faith it is impossible to please and be satisfactory to Him. For whoever would come near to God must [necessarily] believe that God exists and that He is the rewarder of those who earnestly and diligently seek Him [out].
>
> —HEBREWS 11:6, AMP

At this season it is important that you believe that God is actively engaged in every detail of your life and that He will reward you if you are continually pursuing Him.

God has a call for your life, but you must be ready and willing to act according to His times and seasons. As you move forward in your God-given destiny, persevering, capitalizing, and maximizing every season, you will develop the capacity to walk as a modern-day Deborah in the earth. You will be like Deborah the Issacharite, discerning the time and seasons of your life and gaining wisdom on what to do.

Prayer to Activate the Timing of the Lord

Lord, I pray that You will make me a woman who understands time and seasons. Enlighten the eyes of my understanding. Help me balance the seasons of my life.

There is a season and time to every purpose. Thank You, Lord, for the Issachar anointing. Lord, I want to do to everything You've assigned to my life. Let the spirit of revelation and understanding be released in my life.

I decree that I am a woman who walks in total synchronization with the time clock of heaven. I loose myself from time-delay spirits. I decree divine acceleration in my life. I will no longer lag behind, neither will I get ahead of You. I will be in the right place at the right time.

I decree divine alignment for my assignment. I decree alignment in my thought patterns. I decree alignment in my time. I will not squander time. I will maximize every moment for the purposes of the Lord.

Lord, I give You permission to remove anything that will delay Your purposes in my life. Remove anything that will hinder Your call on my life, including relationships or people. Let me attract the people who will propel me into Your purposes for my life. Lord, send instructors and mentors who have words of wisdom and instructions in due season for my life.

Thank You, Lord, for appointing my days and ordering my steps. I surrender to Your timing. In Jesus's name, I pray. Amen.

Chapter 2

DEBORAH: THE JUDGE AND DELIVERER

> Now Deborah, the wife of Lappidoth, was a prophetess. She judged Israel at that time.
>
> —JUDGES 4:4

I HAVE A confession to make: My name is Michelle McClain-Walters, and I hated women's ministry. There, I got it off my chest. I know *hate* is a strong word, but my first experience with women's ministry was something out of a horror movie. I was attending a women's prayer conference, and the women were yelling at the top of their voices as if someone was stabbing them repeatedly. One person took the microphone and began to yell, "Run! I said, Run! You better run for your breakthrough!" You would've thought we were at the starting line of the Boston Marathon. Women took off running in every direction! I stood there like a deer in headlights, afraid I might get trampled.

Then the lady with the bull horn, I mean, microphone, looked at me with a sharp disapproving glare and said, "Some people think they are too cute to run. They're afraid of messing up their hair or makeup!"

I said to myself, "No, lady, I'm afraid of you, and I'm in shock because I can't find anywhere in the Bible that running will give you a breakthrough!"

You know what happened next. Yep, she marched right over to me like a fire-breathing dragon and said, "Kneel before the Lord as sign of humility!"

I kept thinking to myself, "You should have just grabbed your stuff and run with the rest of the women but detoured straight out of that door!"

While down there on my knees, I said, "Lord, I came here because I needed some answers for my life and deliverance from this pain in my soul, not for this tomfoolery!"

When I felt that the coast was clear and her focus was on someone else, I slowly got up off the floor, and as I was gathering my things to leave, I heard the Lord say to me, "The things that irritate you are the things you are designed to change. There will come a day when you will bring wise counsel and deliverance to women worldwide. This is a part of the Deborah anointing on your life."

I said, "Lord, I need so much deliverance and freedom. How can I help someone else?"

Many times the Lord will bring identification and definition to the call on your life in the midst of your humiliation and pain. This encounter sent me on a journey to discover who Deborah was and how the anointing on her life related to counsel and deliverance.

One Mantle, Two Functions

> Judge *and* vindicate me, O God; plead and defend my cause against an ungodly nation. O deliver me from the deceitful and unjust man!
>
> —PSALM 43:1, AMP, EMPHASIS ADDED

The Days of the Judges lasted between three and four hundred years, and the issues of that day were chronicled in the Book of Judges. It was a season of moral outrage, a period of gross immorality, lawlessness, and violence, much like our society today. Everyone did what was right in his own eyes, exactly what he wanted, when he wanted, and as he wanted. This resulted in a tragic, comprising, permissive lifestyle of destruction and chaos.

There was no peace, security, or stability in the land. There was only anxiety, danger, corruption, injustice, and death.

Within Israel the task of the judge was more than just determining legal cases. The judge was the leader of the people. The judge was the president or king of the nation. The judge was the military and civil leader. When God raised up a person to become the judge of His people, that person became the savior, deliverer, and liberator of the people, rescuing them from some oppressor. The judge had the responsibility to give wise counsel to God's rebellious people and also bring deliverance from the oppressor. This is the first dimension of Deborah's mantle as judge that she functioned in for twenty years.

Modern-day Deborahs will have an anointing to rise in the midst of great adversity and lead others to liberty and freedom. Many women are in bondage to fear, deception, insecurities, and pain that keep them from moving into the fullness of life the Lord has promised for them. Modern-day oppressors are ungodly beliefs about how God can't anoint and use women in high-level ministry or business. Even still, the enemies we face are more internal than external. Our hearts and minds, unwilling to follow the precepts of the Lord, enslave and stagnate us because of hurts and wounds in our souls. Many women are under demonic oppression and need deliverance. These are days when Jesus is revealing Himself to women as the deliverer.

There is also a great reformation coming to women's ministry. God is calling modern-day Deborahs to take their positions as visionaries and to pioneer a movement of deliverance and empowerment among women. Women's ministry will no longer be a place where we learn about cupcake decorating or run around a building as maniacs looking for breakthrough. These meetings will resemble military boot camps to train God's special agents for the end times. God is calling women who have the Deborah anointing to disciple women in the art of discernment, developing skills to make sound decisions, and, yes, even training women in ministry of deliverance. Women will arise to gather and pray, executing the vengeance of God upon the enemy and against injustice in the earth. He is removing misconception and the insecurity-guided judgments we place on one another. He is breaking down walls of fear and intimidation between women.

Justice Under the Palm Tree of Deborah

> She would sit under the palm tree of Deborah between Ramah and Bethel in the hill country of Ephraim. The children of Israel would go up to her for her to render judgment.
>
> —JUDGES 4:5

The second dimension of Deborah's mantle was to administer sound counsel and settle disputes for the children of Israel. The judge had the responsibility to be a righteous leader in society and government. Deborah was a righteous leader who led and provided guidance for God's people.

Psalm 106:3 says, "How blessed are those who keep justice, who practice righteousness at all times!" (NASB). Counsel and wisdom demonstrated the justice of God. Justice is making wrong things right.

The Hebrew word for justice is *mishpat* and speaks of social order as well as legal equity.[1] The Great Commission is a call to disciple all nations (Matt. 28:19). This transformational mandate involves establishing justice in all of society. Modern-day Deborahs will have skills in the following major areas:

1. Servant-leadership style

2. Discerning of spirits

3. Supernatural wisdom

Can you imagine the conversations that took place under that palm tree? We must remember these people were under oppression because they had left the ways of God. They were practicing idolatry and perversion; the things discussed probably were as bad as a modern reality television show! I am also intrigued that Deborah was under a tree. I believe that her sitting under the tree represents servant leadership. Those who have the Deborah anointing will learn how to spend time with people and minister with compassion to their plights. These women will have strong leadership skills motivated by the heart of the servant. Deborah wasn't in a fancy tent; she was right in the elements with people. The Deborah anointing will involve strong listening skills and the gift of discerning of spirits. Women who operate with the Deborah anointing will have supernatural wisdom to hear the truth behind the story to administer the justice of God. Let's take a closer look at each of these three elements.

Servant-leadership style

The day of the prima donna prophetess is over! The servant-leader will seek to serve God's people, not for God's people to serve them and their agenda. Traditionally leaders have been valued for their communication and decision-making skills. Servant-leaders must reinforce the important skill of listening intently to others. Servant-leaders are interested in the growth and well-being of people. They always serve first, leading from the conscious choice to give of themselves. They seek to listen receptively to what is being said (and not said). Listening to others will help restore value to people in our sphere of influence. Listening and advising will be a unique distinction of the Deborah anointing.

Romans 12:8 discusses the two *motivational* gifts of leadership and compassion. Like spiritual temperaments, the motivational gifts are the reason a certain Christian has zeal for one assignment. Leading involves thriving on organizing, facilitating, and directing. Compassion involves showing mercy that desires to heal and advocate for hurting hearts. The uniqueness of the Deborah anointing will be a combination of these two motivational gifts.

What is the New Testament theology of spiritual gifts and women? God gifts men and women with natural abilities; God helps men and women to acquire leadership skills; and God gifts both men and women with spiritual gifts. There is no gender prerequisite with God as it relates to leading and power. God gives grace to whomever is humble. It is by His grace that either men or women are gifted for leadership and are able to operate in Holy Spirit power. The New Testament also teaches that those gifted by God are responsible to employ their gifts for one another as good stewards of God's great grace (1 Pet. 4:10).

Discerning of spirits

Spiritual discernment gives one the ability to know and be informed of what is happening in the spiritual realm. Discerning of spirits is supernatural insight into the realm of the spirit. *Discern* means "to separate mixture, to reveal truth." Discernment is not suspicious. It reveals the type of spirit behind a person, a situation, an action, or a message. It is knowing supernatural revelation in the spirit concerning the source, nature, and activity of any spirit.

Both Jesus and Paul used their prophetic giftings to discern spirits. (See Matthew 16:16–23; Acts 16:16–18.) For modern-day Deborahs this spiritual skill is important because the two dominant spirits released against women are seduction and deception. The devil has used these spirits against women since the Garden of Eden.

Supernatural wisdom

The wisdom I am speaking about here is a spiritual gift of the Holy Spirit and much more. The Lord is releasing a supernatural anointing of wisdom, an abiding anointing of wisdom.

God will give you supernatural wisdom for the person on your job who loves to come tell you about her problems, or that millionaire in your circle who doesn't know what to do about her schizophrenic child. You may not be one who preaches messages publicly in the pulpit, but you can preach the best message to someone's life, healing and delivering them through the wisdom of God that flows through you. This is the same wisdom that Solomon had (1 Kings 4:29). Solomon asked God for supernatural wisdom, and He gave it to him. God will release to you this same anointing for supernatural wisdom. You will know things you aren't supposed to know, things you hadn't even studied. He will give you this wisdom by inspiration.

Word of wisdom

It is God's wisdom given to a person so they know to proceed in a course of action based on natural or supernatural knowledge. It's supernatural ability in the Spirit to impart special or specific information, guidance, or counsel, which brings life-changing illumination.

Directional wisdom

This is God telling you what to do, how to do it, and what is going to happen in the future. This is a flash of divine inspiration that is nearly always directed to the future. A great example of directional wisdom is found in Genesis 6:14–18, when the Lord gave Noah divine inspiration and direction for how to build the ark.

Bring It All Together

This is the hour when God is raising up modern-day Deborahs who will administrate the justice of the Lord. They will be empowered by the Holy Spirit with the gifts of wisdom and discerning of spirits. They will administrate justice with the heart of a servant-leader who listens to others to help restore personal value. They will be women who represent a personal God to an impersonal world. They will be women who listen and advise according to the heart and mind of God. They will have spiritual insight from the heart of God to bring deliverance and freedom from decades of oppression from the enemy.

These modern-day Deborahs will have an anointing to settle disputes and foster true kingdom relationships. They will have an understanding heart to discern justice. They will be women who delight in the fear of the Lord. They will not judge by natural sight of their eyes nor decide by the hearing of natural ears. But with true spiritual skills, they will rule with equity and righteousness. They will be women who have ears that are open and tongues that are bridled, walking in the wisdom of the Spirit to bring change to their spheres of influence.

If this sounds like the spirit of a woman God is creating and refining in you, begin to use these prayers as a starting point in your time with God and allow Him to release these gifts into every area of your life.

Prayer to Release the Gift of Leadership

Lord, I ask that You will awaken the gift of leadership inside me. I desire to lead Your people with all diligence, righteousness, and integrity. Let me be a leader who represents You and Your character. Let me be a leader who speaks the truth in love, meeting the needs of Your people. (See Romans 12:8.)

Let my life reflect the holy standard of the kingdom. Give me the grace to stand in front of Your people leading them with Your heart and mind.

Let Your anointing and grace rest on me to speak words of encouragement, correction, direction, vision, and purpose. Give me eyes to see the potential You've placed inside Your people. Give me wisdom to direct them to path of righteousness. Give me insight to instruct and train them to be mighty warriors with hearts to serve Your purposes.

Prayer to Activate the Gift of Discerning of Spirits

Lord, Your Word declares that if I ask You for a gift, You will give it to me. So, Lord, I ask You for the gift of discerning of spirits. Let the supernatural power of the Holy Spirit be activated in me to detect the realm of the spirits and their activities. Let me have a grace to discern between good and evil. Let me have spiritual insight to Your plans and supernatural revelation of plans of the enemy. Empower me with Your supernatural ability to discern and stop the plans of the enemy against my life and the lives of others. Give me a wise and understanding heart that I might discern justice. (See Matthew 7:7–11; James 1:17; 1 Kings 3:9–11.)

Prayer to Activate the Gift of the Word of Wisdom

Lord, I ask for the gift of the word of wisdom. I want to be a woman of wisdom who responds to situations under Your divine direction. Let me have supernatural perspective to accomplish Your will in every situation. Give me words of wisdom to apply the knowledge given to me by Your Spirit.

Lord, I pray that You will give me wisdom to rightly judge Your people. Let my heart perceive and understanding Your ways. Let me not be deceived by crafty and wicked people. Holy Spirit, I ask that You will lead me into all truth. (See 1 Kings 4:29–30; John 14:26; 16:13.)

Chapter 3

DEBORAH THE MOTHER

But understand this, that in the last days will come (set in) perilous times of great stress and trouble [hard to deal with and hard to bear]. For people will be lovers of self and [utterly] self-centered, lovers of money and aroused by an inordinate [greedy] desire for wealth, proud and arrogant and contemptuous boasters. They will be abusive (blasphemous, scoffing), disobedient to parents, ungrateful, unholy and profane.

—2 TIMOTHY 3:1–2, AMP

I COULDN'T BELIEVE what my ears were hearing on the evening news. A mother delivers a baby in a toilet, kills the baby, and returns to the prom! What kind of insanity is that? If you're like me, some things you have to read for yourself. Read the story here:

> The New Jersey teen-ager who gave birth in a bathroom stall at her senior prom was charged with murder today after the authorities concluded that she had delivered a healthy boy, cut the umbilical cord, choked him and put him in a plastic bag that she knotted and threw away.
>
> The woman, Melissa Drexler, 18, of Forked River, was charged after an autopsy determined she had choked the baby and smothered him either with her hands or with the plastic bag, said John Kaye, the Monmouth County Prosecutor.
>
> In the midst of it, Mr. Kaye said today, a girlfriend

who had heard sounds from the bathroom stall asked
Miss Drexler if she felt ill. The Prosecutor said she
replied: "'I'll be done pretty soon. Go tell the boys we'll
be right out.'"

A few minutes later, leaving blood on the floor of the
bathroom stall, Miss Drexler went to the dance floor
with her boyfriend and prom date, John Lewis, ate a
salad and danced one dance.[1]

There are many more stories like this of mothers killing their
babies, leaving them in hot cars for an entire day and causing
them to suffocate, shaking them to death, or, even worse, aborting
them. When did mothers become so self-centered and lovers of
themselves and pleasure?

Many times, as a modern-day Deborah, I receive burdens to
pray through a news story that awakens my heart of compassion. I sometimes ask the Lord how He feels about certain events,
such as the above-mentioned incident. This will oftentimes open
a channel of communication between the Lord and me.

One of the major responsibilities of a modern-day Deborah
is to bring the heart and mind of God in the earth. When I
questioned the Lord about what is happening with these young
girls, I heard Him say, "The battlefield is no longer a threat to
the next generation. The real threat in the twenty-first century is
the wombs of young women." Abortion is a serious issue in our
society, but the bigger, underlying problem is that the power of
nurture is missing in the hearts of women.

Women are called to nurture life. God called Eve the mother
of all living things. Her role was to nourish and nurture all living
things. Women are life givers not life takers. Abortion is a result
of perversion in the hearts of women.

The mothering anointing includes the ability to teach and
train. The mothering anointing must be restored in the earth. We

must become nonconformists. We must be transformed by the renewing of our minds. We must train our daughters according to biblical principles even when it's not popular.

Deborah had the heart of a mother. This was what primarily motivated her leadership over the people of Israel—her rulings, strategies, and interactions with them. Her ability to persevere against all odds was rooted in her desire to nurture village life. Her prophetic insight and powerful intercession was motivated by a mother's love for legacy. For Deborah did not see greatness in emulating the qualities of manhood, but with kindness and faith she sought to be a mother in Israel, a giver of life, and a nurturer of her people.

"Mother" was the title she gave herself. So not only was she a judge, warrior, wife, prophetess, and worshipper, she was also a dispenser and wellspring of life. Her lifestyle is a lesson for our own generation, for all women looking to define themselves and fully use their potential. Being a mother in Israel illuminated the grace and foundation of Deborah's strength and wisdom.

Mothering is so needed in today's Christian community. The spiritually immature need the wisdom of the wiser, older believers. Mothering is life-giving and life-changing. Mothering is mentoring.

When you meet with someone on a regular basis, you are investing in that person. As you do this, you continue to elevate and help them grow to a higher place. So many people get to a certain point and feel that what they are is all they can be. A mentor is placed in their lives to help them climb higher.

We must recover and restore the ancient paths. There must be a recapturing of the essence of motherhood. We must be intentional about training our daughters to be godly mothers in the kingdom. *To nurture* involves "the act of nursing." It means "to suckle or nourish." It also means "to further the development of."[2] God designed the human nature to be nurtured by a mother and a father. The dismantling of the family unit was the beginning of the decline of morality in our nation. Nurturing is essential for the health of humanity.

I believe we have to redeem and esteem the essence of the nurturer in our culture. Many in this generation suffer from an *un*nurtured nature. *Nature* can be defined as the innate or essential qualities or character of a person. *Nature* also includes the general psychological characteristics, feelings, and behavioral traits of humankind, regarded as shared by all humans.

Nurture can be defined as the care and attention given to someone or something that is growing or developing. It means upbringing training as in the scripture that says, "Train up a child in the way he should go, and when he is old he will not depart from it" (Prov. 22:6). It's the sum of the environmental factors influencing the behavior and traits expressed by a child. Modern-day Deborahs will be like teachers who nurture the next generation's creativity. They will understand that in order to produce good fruit in our children, they must carefully nurture the vine.

A New Expression of God in Leadership

The Book of Judges highlighted many unique character traits about the judges along with the uncommon anointing and unconventional weapons God equipped them with to destroy their enemies. Let's take a look at some of these:

- Ehud was a left-handed man, who, with stealth and agility, put to death King Eglon, an enemy of the people of Israel. (See Judges 3:12–21.)
- Gideon had his army decreased to three hundred. Less was more in this divinely orchestrated war strategy. (See Judges 7.) This band of three hundred men was a unique strategy of war, when military

strength was usually seen in large numbers of troops and many weapons.

+ Othniel had divinely inspired military strategies. (See Judges 3:7–11.)

+ Samson had supernatural strength and the anointed jawbone of a donkey. (See Judges 13–16.)

The nature of almighty God is referenced in each of these accounts of deliverance. God expresses Himself as the almighty deliverer of His people. In the stories of all of the judges before and after Deborah, the Bible talks about their mighty military capabilities against Israel's enemies under the anointing of almighty God. A common expression preceded many of their actions: "Spirit of the Lord came upon him." Yet when it speaks about Deborah, prophetic influence and motherly advice seems to be the focus. (See Judges 4:5–6, 14; 5:7–9.)

Deborah was a godly leader who led by inspiration. I believe her servant-leadership style convinced her followers to extend themselves beyond their own vision. By appointing a woman to lead Israel at this point in the history of the judges, God wanted His people to be exposed to a motherly and feminine influence. This didn't mean that she was weaker or less authoritative; it simply means that her leadership was delivered in a different way.

I like to call her the velvet glove. Modern-day Deborahs will be like a velvet glove. This idiom is used to describe a person who appears gentle but is determined and inflexible underneath. Modern-day Deborahs will be gentle in disposition when dealing with the broken, bruised, and battered, but they will have fists of steel when dealing with enemies of God.

When God rose up Deborah to be a judge, He was introducing us to another expression of leadership. A unique dimension of His attributes is as El Shaddai, mighty and powerful but loving and nourishing. This anointing is solely reserved for women.

It is most profitable to take the term *Shaddai* by itself, seeing it is so rich in spiritual significance. It occurs thirty-one times in the Old Testament and is translated "Almighty." It comes from the root *shad*, which means "breast" or "the blessing of the breast." This why I believe this expression of God is reserved solely for women. Seeing *Shaddai* in these terms presents God as the One who nourishes, supplies, and satisfies.[3]

> The etymological signification of Almighty God (El Shaddai) is both interesting and touching. God (El) signifies the "Strong One" (*See Scofield* "Genesis 1:1"). The qualifying word Shaddai is formed from the Hebrew word "shad," the breast, invariably used in Scripture for a woman's breast....Shaddai therefore means primarily "the breasted." God is "Shaddai," because He is the Nourisher, the Strength-giver, and so, in a secondary sense, the Satisfier, who pours himself into believing lives. As a fretful, unsatisfied babe is not only strengthened and nourished from the mother's breast, but also is quieted, rested, satisfied, so El Shaddai is that name of God which sets Him forth as the Strength-giver and Satisfier of His people.[4]

Women of God, we must allow the Lord to use our motherly qualities in this hour. Deborah gives us an example of consistency of character, love for people, and sound judgment in her roles as prophetess and judge. Through these nurturing attributes, she earned her influence. When everything was on the line, she had the trust of the people that she needed to lead well. There isn't a single instance in the story of Deborah where a man challenged her authority, refused to take her counsel, or rejected the edicts she handed down. It was her motherly love and ability to empathize with others that gave her authority and influence with the rulers and other leaders in her sphere.

In Judges 5:9 Deborah states, "My heart is with the rulers of Israel who offered themselves willingly among the people." Here we read the words that reveal how this was a woman who loved from the heart and was accepted; she recognized her co-laborers for their special and unique spirits.

This is the hour when the Lord will use you like Deborah to be a model of integrity and courage. The Bible says that after Deborah led the people of Israel to victory over Sisera, the land rested for forty years. This was twice as long as any other judge during the Days of the Judges.

Women are essential to the Lord's church. Congregations with women who are active, willing, and harmonious are growing and accomplishing great things for God!

Prayer for Your Gifts to Arise in the Church

Lord, I pray that You will show me my place in the church. Let me discover my unique talents and gifts that I may arise and become active in building Your church and advancing Your purposes in the earth. Let me be a woman of courage and boldness, who speaks Your truth in love. Let me disciple and train the next generation of godly women. Let me be intentional about reproducing a generation of women who are feminine and powerful.

Let me be a woman of grace and dignity. Let me model a woman who is constant and steadfast in the work of the kingdom.

Father, help me develop sound wisdom and judgment in everything I do. Increase my influence; let my voice be heard in this hour.

A Mother's Prayer for the Next Generation

Lord, I pray that Your purpose for the next generation will be fulfilled. I decree that the next generation will arise in power, authority, and influence to possess the gates of their enemies. (See Genesis 22:17–18.)

I bind all spirit of premature death and destruction. I decree long life over the next generation.

I pray for academic excellence and social impact to rest upon the next generation. I decree that the next generation of Christian leaders will resist all false doctrines such as humanism, secularism, and hedonism. They will know the truth, preach the truth, and live out the truth of the Lord Jesus. (See Daniel 1:4–5.)

I decree that the seed of the righteous shall be delivered from all wicked and ungodly attractions at work to seduce into an alternative lifestyle. (See Proverbs 11:21.)

Lord, I ask that You will encounter the next generation with dreams and visions and an overwhelming awareness of Your love and presence.

Let peace blanket their hearts and minds. Let the God of peace crush fear under their feet. (See Isaiah 54:13–14.)

I decree that next generation will grow in the ways of God. Let them be strengthened in spiritual things. I decree that the next generation will increase in wisdom, stature, and favor of God. (See Luke 2:40, 52.)

I decree that the next generation will be like arrows of the Lord. They will bring forth deliverance to the nations of the earth. (See Psalm 127:3–5.)

Lord, I ask that You will preserve the heritage of the gospel through the next generation! In Jesus's name, I pray. Amen.

Chapter 4

DEBORAH THE WORSHIPPING WARRIOR

On that day, Deborah and Barak son of Abinoam sang: "When the leaders in Israel lead, when the people freely volunteer, bless the LORD! Hear, O kings! Listen, O rulers! I will sing to the LORD; I will sing praise to the LORD God of Israel.

—JUDGES 5:1–3

WE MUST RESTORE the first commandment to the first place, which is to love the Lord your God with all of your heart, mind, soul, and strength. (See Exodus 20:3–7; Matthew 22:37.) The presence of the Lord must become the primary desire of our hearts. Deborah was a passionate worshipper of the Lord. The entire fifth chapter of Judges is a song of praise and adoration to the Lord for deliverance and victory.

Modern-day Deborahs must cultivate a lifestyle of praise and worship before operating in the Deborah anointing. Worship is the key that will unlock the warrior in you. The Lord is a man of war (Exod. 15:1–3). Worship is the place the Lord prepares you for war. This is the place you will receive strength and help.

We must develop a devotional life filled with worship. The task ahead for women is great. We must be equipped with spiritual weapons to defeat the enemies of our destiny.

In this chapter I will give some practical steps on practicing the presence of the Lord. I also believe that songwriting and creativity is being birthed in this hour and is a part of the Deborah anointing. Deborah drew her confidence from her relationship with God. God gave her the strategies for the battle with Sisera, and she didn't lose sight of this even in the heat of the battle.

Judges 4:14 says, "And Deborah said to Barak, 'Up! For this is the day in which the LORD has delivered Sisera into your hand. Does not the LORD go out before you?'" (ESV). After the battle was finished, she and Barak wrote and sang a victory song in which they repeatedly thanked God. Women with the Deborah anointing will acknowledge God for His saving presence and protection for their lives.

The song of Deborah stands out as unique in that it celebrates a military victory achieved by two women: Deborah and Jael. It provides a glimpse of how God defeated Canaan: God brought a flash flood that made sliding mud in which chariots were useless. On Mount Tabor Deborah the prophet announced the victory. Deborah didn't just write songs of worship; she also lived a life of worship! It's as though every event in her life was used as an offering and sacrifice to God! Deborah used her life as an instrument of worship to God.

Deborah and Barak also worshipped God publicly, using their song to give glory and credit to almighty God for all their successes. Through song they directed the nation to turn its heart to the true and living God. Deborah used praise to inspire, predict, and celebrate. Her weapon of war was her voice. She used her words as an instrument of war. She acknowledged the source of victory. Praise and worship will recalibrate our minds and hearts to focus on the true and living God.

Deborah's actions are a reminder to women that we should not fight in our own strength. She provides a prophetic picture, opens the veil, and reveals a true description of the battle. It is important to remember that God fought: God distressed Sisera. Deborah announced God's victory, Barak facilitated it, and God saved Israel.

Unlike the battles in the Old Testament, New Testament warfare is solely spiritual. Deborah and Barak's natural battle is a shadow and type of the spiritual battle today. Women of God, we will face opposition, but we must learn that the battle is the Lord's. Apostle Paul reminds us of the true enemy of our calling and completing our assignment in the earth. Paul said, "For our fight is not against flesh and blood, but against principalities, against powers, against the rulers of the darkness of this world, and against spiritual forces of evil in the heavenly places" (Eph. 6:12). We must always keep in mind that our real enemy is the devil.

This great battle between the devil and women began in the Garden of Eden. The Lord declared that He would put enmity between women and Satan (Gen. 3:15). *Enmity* can be defined as extreme hatred. There is grace being released upon women to discern and destroy the works of the true enemy of our destiny—the devil. Our problem has never been men or tradition or a glass ceiling, but the spiritual forces that motivate them. This revelation will keep us focused on the mission God has given us to destroy the works of the devil.

Further, Paul said that "the weapons of our warfare are not carnal, but mighty through God to the pulling down of strongholds" (2 Cor. 10:4). You cannot fight a spiritual enemy with natural weapons. We must use spiritual weapons of war to overcome our spiritual enemy. Praise and worship are those weapons. They are spiritual weapons of war that bind and break the powers of darkness.

Our praises will execute God's vengeance.

> Let the high praises of God, be in their mouth, and a two-edged sword in their hand; to execute vengeance upon the heathen, and punishments upon the people; to bind their kings with chains, and their nobles with fetters of iron; to execute upon them the judgment

written; this honour have all his saints. Praise ye
the LORD.

—PSALM 149:6–9, KJV

The Lord admonishes us not to take vengeance or wrath
upon ourselves. God takes vengeance on our behalf, for He said,
"Vengeance is Mine" (Rom. 12:19). Praise and worship usher in
the presence of God, and they play a vital role in destroying the
wicked works of darkness that attempt to come against our lives.
Psalm 68:2 states that the wicked perish in the presence of the
Lord. God wants to bring justice for women in all matters and
give just recompense to whom it is due. With high praises and
the Word of God, which is referred to as the two-edged sword,
we have the ability to execute God's vengeance, bind kings and
nobles, and execute judgments. The primary target of that vengeance is the devil.

The entire account of Judges 5 is deliberately written to empha-
size the deliverance provided by God. Deborah proclaims that
He is the One pulling the strings, raising generals, deploying
armies (even the enemy is indirectly controlled by Him), dic-
tating strategy, and affecting the victory. In the end the song celebrates the saving work of God. Through song Deborah stressed
God's sovereignty over human events.

I believe the Lord will raise up women who will write songs
that glorify the mighty acts of God. Like Deborah, these women
will write and compose songs that will admonish a rebellious
people to turn their hearts to God. This passage also encourages
women to perceive God's sovereignty over history and our own
lives. Whether it is in His compassionate deliverance, financial
provision, or leading and guiding decisions, God is sovereign over
life, and He is at work bringing His plan to fruition in our lives.
By spending time in praise and worship, women will destroy the
enemy and gain the courage to lead in the kingdom of God.

Cultivating the Heart of a Worshipper

Believe me, woman, the time is coming when you Samaritans will worship the Father neither here at this mountain nor there in Jerusalem. You worship guessing in the dark; we Jews worship in the clear light of day. God's way of salvation is made available through the Jews. But the time is coming—it has, in fact, come— when what you're called will not matter and where you go to worship will not matter.

It's who you are and the way you live that count before God. Your worship must engage your spirit in the pursuit of truth. That's the kind of people the Father is out looking for: those who are simply and honestly themselves before him in their worship. God is sheer being itself—Spirit. Those who worship him must do it out of their very being, their spirits, their true selves, in adoration.

—JOHN 4:21–24, THE MESSAGE

Worship is a verb. Worship is about encountering God in a personal and transforming way. We are told in John 4:23–24 that God is spirit and that the true worship the Father is seeking is done in both spirit *and* truth. The correct elements of worship must be a combination of reverence toward God and the truth of God's will.

Worshipping God in spirit involves seeing God with the eyes of our heart. It is adoration and exaltation of someone greater than you. In adoration we express our delight and total confidence in God. Worship comes from the Latin word that translates as "worth-ship." It literally means to ascribe worth to something.

True worship begins with a deep respect or reverence for God, a frame of heart, an attitude. This must be fixed in one's mind before we go further. An "act" of worship is an act proceeding from or the result of that attitude. Worship demands nothing less than the complete, conscious, and intentional participation of the believer. We need to understand that the blessings we receive from worship are a by-product of our worship and not the focus. In worship we come to do and give, not receive. Worship is first and foremost about God. Worship is about the creation encountering the Creator.

The Hebrew word for worship is *shachah*, and it means "to bow, to stoop; to bow down before someone as an act of submission or reverence; to worship; to fall or bow down when paying homage to God. The primary meaning is 'to make oneself low.'...worship (bow yourselves down low before Him) at the place of His feet."[1]

In the New Testament the Greek word *proskyneō* especially denotes homage rendered to God and the ascended Christ. *Proskyneō* comes from *pros*, meaning "toward," and *kyneo*, meaning "to kiss." We can deduce the full meaning of the Greek expression for worship as to prostrate oneself, bow down, do obeisance, show reverence, do homage, worship, adore.[2] All believers have a one-dimensional worship, which is to the only Lord and Savior. We do not worship angels, saints, shrines, relics, or religious personages. When we prostrate ourselves in worship, we place our lives before God.

> So here's what I want you to do, God helping you: Take your everyday, ordinary life—your sleeping, eating, going-to-work, and walking-around life—and place it before God as an offering. Embracing what God does for you is the best thing you can do for him. Don't become so well-adjusted to your culture that you fit into it without even thinking. Instead, fix your attention on God. You'll be changed from the inside out. Readily recognize what he wants from you, and quickly respond to it. Unlike the culture around you, always dragging

you down to its level of immaturity, God brings the best
out of you, develops well-formed maturity in you.

—ROMANS 12:1–2, THE MESSAGE

Worship Destroys Fear and
Produces Confidence in God

One of the biggest enemies to the call of God is fear of man.
The Bible states that the fear of man brings a snare in our lives
(Prov. 29:25). The psalmist proclaims, "I sought the LORD, and
He answered me, and delivered me from all my fears" (Ps. 34:4).
There will be times during the process of walking in your calling
that the enemy will try to fill your heart with fear. Many women
are plagued with the fear of not being good enough to fulfill all
the demands of life. The presence of the Lord—worship—is
where fears are destroyed.

One of the greatest monsters that I wrestle with in my leadership is being confident in the calling and gifting God has for me.
I battle insecurity, fear, and the obsessive need to compare myself
to others. These enemies to my confidence can get the best of me
if I let them.

Comparison and competition are enemies to the call of
God. We usually take our weakness and compare it to someone
else's strength, and this causes us to be insecure and fearful.
The only thing that can cast out the spirit of fear is the love of
God, for the perfect love of God casts out every spirit of fear.
Worship is the place where love is perfected and peace of mind is
restored. Perfected love casts out fear, for there is no fear in love
(1 John 4:18).

Woman of God, we must learn to fear God over man. The
fear of the Lord must be our pursuit in this hour. We put God
in His rightful place in our lives when we worship Him. This
is why worship must be a lifestyle for the modern-day Deborah.
Worship cannot be limited to a church service. It should be part

of everything we do every hour of every day. This is when God is high and lifted up for us to see Him and see His perspective on what He has called us to do. Worship allows us to know His thoughts and desire to please Him in reverence and in holy fear.

> Who is the [woman] who fears the LORD? He will teach [her] in the way He should choose. [She] will dwell at ease, and [her] descendants will inherit the land. The counsel of the LORD is with those who fear him, and He will make His covenant known to them. My eyes are ever toward the LORD, for He will lead my feet from the net.
>
> —PSALM 25:12–15

Worship Gives You Confidence to Go to War

> LORD, when You went out from Seir, when You marched from the land of Edom, the ground shook and the skies poured, indeed, the dense clouds poured water.
>
> —JUDGES 5:4

Deborah received a revelation of God in the place of worship. She understood that she was not in the battle alone. In fact, she had a revelation of God as El Shaddai, the God who compels nature to do what is contrary to itself. Judges 5 gives us an account of what actually happened on the battlefield. It was the Lord who went out to fight, and heaven responded when Deborah arose. The almighty God caused it to rain rendering Sisera and his nine hundred chariots powerless. Worship caused the rain of heaven to fall. (See Zechariah 14:17.) Women with the Deborah anointing will learn the art of worship that causes rain to fall from heaven.

Worship is also the place where you become a bond slave to the Lord and the cry of your heart is "Send me; I will go." This is where Deborah received her courage to say to Barak, "I will go with you to war." She received her confidence to go and warn through worship. Worship brought her into the secret place of the Most High.

Deborah abided under the shadow of the Almighty (El Shaddai). I believe she had a revelation of God's eternal, miraculous power combined with His supreme sufficiency. The revelation of the "almightiness" of God gave her the faith to face anything and the ability inspire others.

Worship takes you to the mountain of the Lord to see life from His perspective. Before the Fall, communion was a natural part of human existence, part of the rhythm of life. God has always desired that this rapport, this rhythm, be restored. Worship is communing with God. In the place of worship is where we learn God's thoughts and receive His embrace.

Keys to Dwelling in the Secret Place

> He who dwells in the secret place of the Most High shall remain stable and fixed under the shadow of the Almighty [Whose power no foe can withstand].
>
> —PSALM 91:1, AMP

I have often wondered where the secret place of God was. Through revelation and study, I've come to believe that the secret place is the sanctuary, or temple, of God.

> What? Do you not know that your body is the temple of the Holy Spirit, who is in you, whom you have received from God, and that you are not your own?
>
> —1 CORINTHIANS 6:19

We learn from these scriptures that when we receive Christ's free gift of salvation, the Lord makes His sanctuary within us. His Holy Spirit then dwells within that inner sanctuary and teaches us, directs us, tells us, and reveals to us the greater things of God.

The word *dwells* in Psalm 91:1 is *yashab* which means "to dwell, remain, sit, abide."[3] The key to receiving protection and guidance is to stay in the secret place, under the shadow of the Most High. Dwelling in the secret place involves the concepts listed below:

+ Listening: We must learn to quiet our noisy minds and open our spiritual ears to hear God's voice. Learning to discern God's voice takes time in worship and prayer and becoming a student of the Word.

+ Watching: Behold the beautiful God and develop a sharp vision and understanding of God's heart and His purpose for this generation. I believe Deborah spent hours in the presence of the Lord. Some scholars believe she spent hours in the temple lighting lamps for the Lord, symbolic of waiting on the Lord. The rabbis say she employed herself in making wicks for the lamps of the tabernacle before becoming judge in Israel.[4] She spent many hours in the presence of the Lord before the time of her promotion to a leadership position.

+ Waiting: This is a rare virtue that will determine how well we listen and watch. Waiting on the Lord kills the flesh. Waiting also means to serve or minister to the Lord.

+ Finding: This occurs when you begin to experience and encounter the living God, feeling His affections and emotions and discovering His passion for you. As women, we must all find time to dwell in the secret place with the Lord. When we behold Him, we begin to find ourselves. In the presence of the Lord you will feel the fire of His love for you, making it easy to share with others. Psalm 16:11 states that God will show us the path of life and in His presence is the fullness of joy. When finding God in the secret place, we find our path in life.

Revelation in Worship

Today a new sound is coming forth. God is raising up women with the anointing of Deborah who will write songs to bring revelation of the heart and mind of God to the church. These songs will teach and admonish us with the truths concerning principles of the kingdom of God. God is raising up prophetic songwriters to bring forth songs of the Spirit that will turn the heart of a generation back to Him.

Whenever the Lord wants to implement a new season, He commands a new song to be sung. He raises up psalmists to write songs that embody the truths of His heart. He enhances every revelation through the use of music and worship. In Song of Songs 2:11–12 it says, "For now the winter has past; the rain is over and gone. The flowers appear on the earth; the time of singing has come." This scripture speaks of the wind of change blowing throughout the earth to usher in fresh insight, revelation, and experiences, accompanied by new songs and expressions of worship.

Through worship, we enter into the presence of the Lord, and we are welcomed to a new place where we can see life from His perspective. In worship God reveals new aspects of Himself to us. Knowing that God is enthroned on our praises (Ps. 22:3), we then proceed to find out the character and nature of Him for whom we are preparing a habitation. The word *enthroned* means to install a king on a throne, especially during a ceremony to mark the beginning of their rule. It also means to seat someone in a position of authority, sovereign power, and rule.

Wherever God's people exalt His name, He is ready to manifest His kingdom power. Our praise and worship prepares a specific place and position for God to reign in our lives.

True worship will always bring balance and resolve. Women can sometimes be unbalanced in this area. We can spend so much time in worship soaking in His presence that we become waterlogged. We just fixate on the experience of being in His presence and end up worshipping the experience and not God. Then there are others who are so focused on destroying the enemy that they become fanatical and even delusional.

God desires for women to be balanced and whole. God desires to reveal Himself to us as Redeemer. God has a purpose for His manifest presence, which is there to minister to us and through us. His purpose is that we may know Him intimately, find His path for our lives, find joy and pleasure in His presence, and minister to mankind from His perspective.

Prayer to Dwell in the Presence of the Lord

Lord, in Your presence is the fullness of joy! I ask that You will draw me by Your Spirit into the secret chambers of Your love. I desire to know You. I desire to know Your ways and plans for my life. Lord, You are my refuge and my fortress. My God, in You do I trust. I set my affections and love upon You. I draw nigh to You, and You draw nigh to me.

Show me Your path for my life. I trust You with my whole heart, leaning not on my understanding. I search for Your wisdom. I choose to delight myself in You, and You will give me the desires of my heart. I cast all of my cares upon You for You care for me. Lord, You are my strong fortress that I run to, and I am safe. Amen.

Chapter 5

DEBORAH THE HONEYBEE

> The fact that I am a woman does not make me a different kind
> of Christian, but the fact that I am a Christian does make me
> a different kind of woman.[1]
>
> —Elisabeth Elliot

Beautiful women are a dime a dozen, but godly women are extremely rare. The world suffers the loss of godly feminine qualities such as trust, modesty, grace, ladylike innocence, tenderness, patience, and love.

I remember when I was growing up people would say to me in a corrective tone of voice, "Stop crying like a girl. You're such a girly girl. You need to toughen up."

My response was, "News flash, genius, I am a girl! And I won't apologize for it!"

I love being a female. I love wearing my high heels and putting on my makeup and perfume. You could smell me a block away. Oh, and I love to accessorize! The more glitter and rhinestones the better! I think I was the only one in the fifth grade who carried a purse and wore high heels. I love being feminine and all the qualities it includes. I love to encourage, nurture, and add value to those around me. Even in high school I was a defender of the young and a voice for the voiceless. I remember my friends saying to me, "Michelle, you think you're everybody's mama!"

No one taught me how to be feminine; it was an innate ability. At a young age I identified with the essence of my femininity. It was who God created me to be!

A woman in her glory is a woman who is not striving to become feminine or ladylike. She knows the core of her being where God dwells and that He created her as a woman.

I'm not here to tell you that there are one hundred one rules for being feminine. You don't have to polish your nails and get a facial in order to be feminine. Although, if you've never tried it, you should. However, you can be feminine without doing these things. You are also not immediately feminine just because you wear dresses and high heels.

Our heroine Deborah's rich legacy echoes through the annals of time to every woman who can lead in the midst of a male-dominated society and still be feminine. There was a time in the not-too-distant past when women had to take on more masculine character traits and mannerisms in order to be considered equal to men. There were books, seminars, and magazine articles to help us achieve this. But no more. God did not design us this way. Just because we are different doesn't make us any less valuable.

Femininity is power and authority under control. Deborah's lifestyle is a lesson for all women who are looking to define themselves and fully use their potential. You can be gentle and assertive. You can inspire and not intimidate.

Deborah calls herself a "mother in Israel." She took her role of mother over her people very seriously and faithfully. She followed God and led her children, the Israelites, to put their faith in the Lord to deliver them from their enemies. Deborah held the highest spiritual, political, and military positions during that time of Israel's history, and yet I love the fact that in Judges 5:7 Deborah doesn't refer to herself as judge, prophetess, or leader. She describes herself as "a mother in Israel." She didn't need to prove herself or remind others of her positional power.

If you are a women's leader or an aspiring women's leader in the body of Christ, I want to encourage you to celebrate those feminine qualities because God is going to use them to lead His people just as He did with Deborah.

Words, Sweet Like Honey

Deborah's unique qualities were displayed through her words. The Bible tells us in Job 6:25, "How forceful are right words!" and in Proverbs 18:21, "Death and life are in the power of the tongue." Deborah words calmed the weary, advised the lost, inspired a general, and moved a nation to war.

God's anointed weapons of choice for women are words. Psalm 119:103 says, "How sweet are Your words to the taste of my mouth! Sweeter than honey to my mouth!" The name *Deborah* means "bee because it signifies the law like honey in the wax; that is, it contains in the letter the sweetness of the Spirit." [2] Deborah's very name is the key to understanding her. The essence of her name, "honeybee," is the essence of the anointing that will rest upon women. Just as bees swarm behind a leader, women will have new leadership responsibilities in the church and will be recognized as prophets who teach and guide the body of Christ. The sting of the bee is bitterly painful, yet its honey is sweet, so will women who have godly dispositions, demonstrate sweet words of wisdom to those they influence and a deadly sting for the enemies of God.

Jewish parents believed the name of a child was instrumental in forming their identity. They believed that the nature, character, and destiny of children should be proclaimed in their name.

> *Deborah* comes from the Hebrew root, meaning to speak or promise. It's also where the phrase "Word of God" comes from and is identical to the word, meaning "bee." [3]

Some commentators believe that the bee was called "a speaker" because of its buzzing. Scholars also suggest that the bee was named for the *dbr*, a Hebrew root, because it produces honey. The name *Deborah* is identical to the word meaning "bee," and both come from the root *dabar*, meaning to speak or pronounce. The root *dabar* generally pertains to speech and specifically intelligent discourse.[4]

The bee brings forth the honey, which in turn has a lot to do with the Word of God metaphorically. Bees like flowers, make honey, speak a language, care for offspring, and are armed. The "speech" of Deborah was holy prophecy, and what could be sweeter than the words of prophecy? Sweetness suggested the image of honey, and bees, after all, make honey.[5]

The Difference Between Honeybees and Wasps

I would like to like to identify the difference between honeybees and wasps as it relates to developing the Deborah anointing. Here's what I discovered from the experts:

> While honeybees can attack when provoked, wasps are naturally more aggressive predators....
>
> Wasps and honeybees are both members of the *Hymenoptera* order of insects. However, their physical bodies are different. Honeybees measure around 2.54 cm long. Some have entirely black bodies, while others are black or brown with orange or yellow striations. Honeybees are hairy, while wasps usually have smooth and shiny skin. Wasps are narrow-waisted, have four wings, and may be brightly colored, with black and yellow patterns.
>
> Wasps and bees also differ in lifestyle and habits. Honeybee colonies can have populations over 75,000, while wasps' colonies tend to have fewer than 10,000 individuals. Queen wasps build a nest for their colony, while worker honeybees create and maintain hives. Unlike most wasps that hibernate during the winter

season and build a new nest the following autumn, honeybees do not hibernate, as they live on food reserves and heat accumulated by thousands of workers. Wasp species cannot produce honey, but all species of honeybees are capable of producing and storing sizeable amounts of honey within their hives. While honeybees can sting only once and die after attacking, a single wasp is capable of stinging multiple times....

Honeybees are social creatures and live within colonies with a queen, thousands of workers and a few male drones. Workers make these nests from wax, which they secrete from their abdominal glands. Within each cell, young workers place pollen and nectar as food for developing larvae. Male drones are ejected from the nest to die during autumn, after they have completed their only task in life: to mate with queens. The age of honeybees also plays an important role in determining which individuals perform various daily activities.[6]

Those who have the Deborah anointing will have an ability like the honeybee to produce honey.

+ "Honey was the chief sweetener in the olden days, and...God's words are sweeter than honey" (Ps. 119:103).[7] Women will have words of encouragement from the heart of God that will bring healing restoration to many in their sphere of influence.

+ "Ezekiel reports that the scroll full of lamentations that God gave him tasted after like honey."[8] Women will have to eat the entire roll of Scripture, which will bring transformation to their hearts. Committing these truths and promises to their hearts will influence their speech. The Word in our hearts is to teach or control our speech and conduct. The "sweetness" and "health" such speech promotes empowers others to overcome and live victorious lives. Those of us with the honeybee anointing will release divine grace in our daily living. The words of revelation will lead the believer to "an overcoming, victorious life, through a consistent acknowledgment of the power and might of God with both mouth and manner." [9]

+ Honey is known for its sweetness and medicinal qualities. Women will have pleasant words and healing anointing to bring wholeness to many who are broken and wounded. The wise words of those with the Deborah anointing will bring health. There is a healing anointing being released on women—the healing anointing with the gift of words of knowledge. "Pleasant words are as a honeycomb, sweet to the soul and health to the bones" (Prov. 16:24).

+ Honey also symbolizes abundance and prosperity. The Promised Land flowed with milk and honey. Women will have an abundance of wisdom that will lead them and others around them to prosperity.

+ Honey is associated with wisdom: "My son, eat honey because it is good, and the honeycomb that is sweet to your taste; so shall the knowledge of wisdom be to your soul; when you have found it, then there will be a reward, and your expectation will not be cut off" (Prov. 24:13–14).

Busy As a Bee

"Busy as a bee" is an idiomatic expression that refers to someone who is deeply engaged in the completion of a task or set of tasks, making use of all his or her resources to bring about the desired end. Typically, a person who is engaged to this degree has neither the time nor the ability to step away and take on some other task until at least some of the current efforts are completed.[10]

Women with the honeybee anointing will be finishers. They will have a grace to start and finish projects. This anointing will empower women in business—women who are industrious or have many things to do; women who are productive, persistent, and focused; and women who are quick to act and like to get things done. I believe this also represents an entrepreneur anointing. This aspect of the Deborah anointing will empower women to develop businesses, giving them power to create wealth.

Those most affected by poverty are women. I declare that the Lord is releasing power to get wealth upon women that they may establish His covenant in the earth. Deuteronomy 8:18 says, "But you must remember the LORD your God, for it is He who gives you the ability to get wealth, so that He may establish His covenant which He swore to your fathers, as it is today." The Hebrew word for "ability" is *koach*; it means "vigor, strength, force, capacity, power, wealth, means, or substance."[11]

> *Koach*...means vigor, strength, force, capacity or ability, whether physical, mental, or spiritual. Here Moses informs Israel that it is God who gives to them the ability (power, means, endurance, capacity) to obtain wealth, for material blessings are included in the promises to the patriarchs and their descendants. Moses strictly warns Israel in [Deuteronomy 18:17] not to falsely conclude that this capacity for success is an innate talent, but to humbly acknowledge that it is a God-given ability.[12]

Women with the Deborah anointing will be effective agitators for change. Have you ever seen a bee come into a room filled with people? That little insect can clear a room in five seconds. Their buzzing around brings agitation to everyone in their vicinity. Modern-day Deborahs will stir up public discussion with their focus set on change. Deborah was an effective agitator for Israel. She stirred up discussion about the low spiritual condition of Israel.

Women with the honeybee anointing will cultivate the following skills and attributes:

- Self-starter
- Motivation
- Resourcefulness
- Organization
- Productiveness
- Teachability
- Adaptability
- Creativity
- Decisiveness
- Persistence
- Results-oriented
- Problem-solving
- Responsibility

Are You a Honeybee or a Wasp?[13]

> These men are grumblers, complainers, who walk after their own lusts. Their mouths speak arrogant words, and they flatter others to gain profit.
>
> —JUDE 16

Women who carry a wasp spirit will not be able to produce honey. They are aggressive and seductive. Their wasplike words carry the sting of bitterness. Their tongues are used for evil speaking and gossip. Evil speaking is also known by ancient rabbis as the "third tongue" because it destroys the speaker.[14] It destroys the one spoken to, and it destroys the one spoken about. It brings great defilement. The Bible tells us it's not what goes into a man that defiles him but what comes out. Those who have a wasp-spirit tongue are like a raging forest fire. This flame is actually fueled by hell. These women with their inappropriate use of the tongue have the potential to morally taint the entire body.

Women should be especially careful about what they speak on and to whom they speak. They represent God in everything they do. The Bible says that out of the abundance of the heart the mouth speaks. This is why the devil will try to nullify the power our greatest warfare weapon against him, which is our God-anointed words, by polluting our hearts. The devil's strategy is to tempt you with sins of the mouth. He attacks women in the speech. How many words have you spoken you wish you could take back? When we initiate or participate in conversation, words can bring defilement on the listener and the person we are speaking about. Sins of the mouth can hinder your expression of femininity. There is the danger of God's righteous wrath for those who continue slanderous, meddling acts. Those with a wasp spirit manifest the following:

- Defilement—to pollute, to make unclean, to tarnish the purity of character by lewdness (Matt. 15:1–19; John 14:30)

- Lewdness—sinning in broad daylight with arrogance and contempt

- Idle words (Matt. 12:33–37)

- Backbiting—one who speaks against an absent individual (Ps. 15:1–3; Rom. 1:28–30)

- Busybody—one who seeks out on a false report and spreads it by means of gossip, slander, and backbiting; a meddler in other people's affairs (1 Pet. 4:15)

- Complaining—grumbling, not loudly but so only those in close proximity can hear

- Slandering—trying to injure someone's reputation or character by sharing damaging stories about the past (Prov. 10:18)

- Talebearing (Lev. 19:16; Prov. 11:13; 17:9; 18:8; 26:20–22)
- Elaborating and exaggerating—making a story more dramatic
- Whispering—privately and secretly talking about other people; mumbling a spell (Prov. 16:28)
- Gossip—casual or unconstrained conversation or reports about other people, typically involving details that are not confirmed as being true.

Steps of Deliverance From the Wasp Spirit

The above-mentioned characteristics have the potential to detour us from the God-ordained path for our lives. Sometimes they can be hidden issues of the heart that only the Holy Spirit can reveal. Women have suffered such cruelty in the world. Many may feel they must use carnal methods to protect themselves and advance in life. Many of these behaviors have become blind spots and can be revealed only by the Holy Spirit. We must develop the discipline of self-examination. Psalm 51 is one of my favorite psalms. Praying it over my life has been a major tool to developing self-examination. David prayed in Psalm 51:6 that God desires truth in the inward parts and in the hidden part He shall make us to know wisdom.

Step 1: Desire truth in your inward parts.

The first step to overcoming the wasp spirit is having a desire for truth in the inward parts. We should desire truth that is not superficial, but truth that reaches far deeper than a mere intellectual comprehension of truth; it is truth that reaches down into the depths our being. The opposite of the truth is deception. The worst kind of deception is self-deception. The power of deception is the person being deceived believes that she is being led of the Lord. It takes the mercy and power of the Holy Spirit to break through deception.

Step 2: Allow the Holy Spirit to search your heart.

The second step to overcoming the wasp spirit is to allow the Holy Spirit to search your heart, shining a light on any wicked area. The Holy Spirit is the Spirit of truth. He will give you wisdom in the hidden areas of your heart. Psalm 139:23–24 says, "Search me [thoroughly], O God, and know my heart! Try me and know my thoughts! And see if there is any wicked or hurtful way in me, and lead me in the way everlasting" (AMP). Once the Holy Spirit searches your heart and reveals blocks and flaws, you must be honest with yourself and not try to justify your actions. David states in Psalm 51:3 that he acknowledged his sins and transgressions. Recognizing sin and error requires humility and brokenness. It's also the first step to healing and deliverance.

Step 3: Repent immediately.

The third step to overcoming the wasp spirit is to immediately repent. Once the Holy Spirit convicts you of having a wasp spirit, there is an anointing in that moment to be healed, delivered, and transformed. Delayed response can lead to hardness of heart and greater deception. *Repent* comes from the Greek word *metanoia*. In this compound word the preposition combines the two meanings of "time" and "change," which may be denoted by "after" and "different"; so that the whole compound means: "to think differently after," "a change of mind accompanied by regret and change of conduct," "a change of mind and heart," or "a change of consciousness."[15] Based on this definition, repentance means, after the Holy Spirit has revealed information, you change your way of thinking. The wrong road will never become the right road. The only way to get on the right road is to discover where you made a detour and turn around immediately.

Step 4: Rend your heart.

The fourth step to overcoming the wasp spirit is to rend the heart. In Joel's day people tore their garments to show their grief and desperation. However, what God desires is the tearing of our hearts, which speaks of dealing radically with the matters of our heart. To *rend* means to tear something violently or forcibly. We tear our hearts away from everything in our lives that quenches or blocks the pure flow of the Spirit! Tearing our hearts is intensely personal and painful. Some want the Spirit to free them from their sinful patterns without it requiring any personal choices that tear their hearts. That is not the way it happens.

> And rend your heart, and not your garments, and turn unto the LORD your God: for he is gracious and merciful, slow to anger, and of great kindness, and repented him of the evil.
>
> —JOEL 2:13, KJV

Women with the Deborah anointing will properly use their tongues. Deborah used hers to speak God's commands to those who needed encouragement to free themselves from oppression. She used cheerful, positive words of victory when God's people faced enemies. Her words were wisely selected, and people traveled far to hear her speak. Women today can imitate Deborah's speech! How often have you seen a woman totally destroy her effectiveness as a leader because she failed to use her tongue properly? (See 1 Timothy 3:11; 5:11–13.) Because of the way Deborah used her tongue, she lifted the spirits of those who needed to be faithful to God.

Prayers for Forcible Words

Lord, Your Word states that right words are forcible. Let me speak words that are appropriate for every occasion. Teach me, Lord, to hold my tongue. Cause me to know where I have erred. I repent for injustice in my tongue. (See Job 6:24–25, 30.) Lord, show me the places where my words have caused confusion, strife,

and division. I ask that You will put Your sweet words
in my mouth that I may bring peace and encouragement to those in my sphere of influence. Let the words
of my mouth and meditations of my heart be pure and
acceptable before You (Ps. 19:14). I pray that You will
create in me a clean heart and renew a righteous spirit
within me (Ps. 51:10). I repent for gossiping, backbiting,
talebearing, and speaking words that defile. I ask, dear
Lord, that as You did with Isaiah, You would take the
coals from Your altar and touch my lips. Let the fire
of the Holy Spirit burn away iniquity in my heart and
purge the sin of my mouth (Isa. 6:6–7). Let my speech
be with grace, seasoned with salt that I will know how
to answer with wisdom (Col. 4:6). Let me be a woman
who is swift to hear, slow to speak, and slow to wrath
(James 1:19).

I decree that my mouth is a well of life! (See Proverbs 10:11.)

I decree that wisdom is found on my lips and I am a
woman of understanding (Prov. 10:13).

I will speak words that edify, exhort, and comfort
those in my sphere of influence (1 Cor. 14:3).

I will speak words of wisdom; my mouth will bring
forth wisdom but the mouth of the perverse will be cut
off (Prov. 10:31).

My tongue will be like the pen of the ready writer,
writing the plans and purpose of God on the hearts of
those I influence (Ps. 45:1).

I will be a woman who restrains my lips and demonstrates wisdom (Prov. 10:19).

My lips will feed many with truth and insight (Prov.
10:21).

Chapter 6

DEBORAH THE PROPHETESS

Surely the Lord GOD does nothing without revealing His purpose to His servants the prophets.

—AMOS 3:7

DEBORAH WAS ONE of the judges of Israel during a time of oppression. As both a judge and a prophetess, she was careful to voice God's will and not her own. She was known for her sound-mindedness and divine justice. God used her to deliver His messages to the people. The Lord spoke through her as she held court under a tree called "the Palm of Deborah" in Ephraim. The Lord also used her to set her people free and defeat the king of Canaan.[1]

Deborah as the prophetess helped to lead God's people out of bondage with precision and accuracy. She stood in the council of the Lord and heard and perceived His word for a generation. She heard and released God's heart and mind to the children of Israel in a time when no one else could hear His voice.

Set Times for a Prophetic Voice

Whenever God has a set time to release His purpose on the earth, He will raise up a prophetic voice. God has an audience to whom He wishes to direct His thoughts. This may be an individual, the church, or the nations. A situation had arisen with the children of Israel that required divine action. His people were in trouble. There was a military threat against the legacy. The people were living in religious compromise and social upheaval.

Rather than figuring out a battle plan against the King of Jabin or putting together a delegation to go negotiate a peace treaty, the Israelites sought the prophetess Deborah to hear the Word of God. This was yet another sign that they were getting back on track spiritually with the Lord. The Israelites were in a serious crisis. Death was literally knocking on their door in the form of a massive army. And rather than rely on their own "knowledge" and strength, they turned to God for a solution. This is so important for Christians today to take heed of. When you face a crisis, tragedy or are terribly afraid, look to God. Turn to the Word or a godly leadership for biblical advice.[2]

When God wants to release His hand of power

Deborah's announcement that Sisera would be destroyed and that deliverance would be given to a woman was a prophetic proclamation of God exerting His power over the enemy nations that oppressed His people. Her words shook the destiny of nations and transformed the strategies of men into the strategies that advanced the kingdom of God. God doesn't release this kind of power without first decreeing it through His servants, the prophets (Amos 3:7).

When God wants to bring hope in times of crisis

In troubled times many people lose their hope, an expectation of good. The plans and the dreams to which they have given their lives can collapse. Often they will feel as if God has abandoned them. Nations will need prophets who can give new vision in these times of transition. Deborah the prophetess had tremendous vision and resolve that came from the heart of the Lord. She explained to Barak how and when it was time to go to battle to break the yoke of the oppressor from the neck of the children of

Israel. Prophets will explain how God is at work in what appears to be a disaster. Prophets can see what is happening in the future plan of God.

Prophetic Dimensions of the Deborah Anointing

The two main dimensions of the Deborah anointing are the spirit of counsel and the spirit of might. I believe the Lord is releasing this grace to women to develop solutions to many problems we're facing all over the world. I believe the Holy Spirit is anointing women with a supernatural anointing of wisdom and might.

The spirit of counsel

The spirit of counsel gives strategy and the ability to devise the right course of action. The prophetess Deborah had the counsel of the Lord for the commander Barak. This ministry of the Spirit of God gives His people direction and guidance concerning God's mind and will. Prophets are required to stand in the counsel of the Lord to hear the voice of God accurately and cause mankind to turn from evil. The premier anointing in the prophet's life should be conviction and the fear of the Lord.

> For who has stood in the counsel of the LORD and has perceived and heard His word? Who has given heed to His word and listened to it?...But if they had stood in My counsel and had caused My people to hear My words, then they would have turned them from their evil way and from the evil of their doings.
> —JEREMIAH 23:18, 22

The word *counsel* is the Hebrew word *cowd*. *Counsel* or *cowd* refers to secret or private counsel, a family circle in which secrets are shared. It also refers to a session or a company of persons in (close deliberation) intimacy—close circle of friends, intimacy with God, to sit down together. Those with a Deborah anointing will cultivate the art of standing in the counsel of the revealer of secrets and mysteries. The term "standing in the counsel of the Lord" means to wait attentively to hear the message that God wants to deliver. Prophets must spend time marking and perceiving the word of the Lord for many of the crises we face today. The Lord has counsel for the mother who has a homosexual son. The Lord has counsel for America's economy. This is the anointing to counsel kings and heads of state and presidents.

The spirit of might

> Then Deborah said to Barak, "Get up, for this is the day that the LORD has given Sisera into your hands. Has not the LORD gone out before you?" So Barak went down from Mount Tabor with ten thousand men behind him. The LORD routed Sisera and all of his chariots and all of his army with the edge of the sword in front of Barak. Sisera dismounted his chariot and fled on foot. Barak chased after the chariots and the army as far as Harosheth Haggoyim. The whole army of Sisera fell by the edge of the sword. Not a single man survived.
>
> —JUDGES 4:14–16

Deborah's bold proclamation to Barak not only caused an entire system of idolatry and oppression to be destroyed, but it also caused the hearts of the people to turn back to God. The spirit of might refers to power and military strength, force, or the impetus to carry out the strategy of the Lord. God is sovereign over the kingdoms of men, and He is leading history. It is the eternal Spirit who reveals to His prophets eternal secrets to rout and destroy the works of darkness. God will watch over His words declared by the prophetess and women who have a prophetic spirit.

Deborah was the prophetess of the Lord. It is an honor and a privilege to be called as a prophet of the Lord. Deborah's primary assignment was to see beyond the present situation and bring the purposes of God into sharp focus. Sisera and his nine hundred chariots appeared to be undefeatable, but the prophetess Deborah could see in the spirit that there were more for the army of Israel than against them. The spirit of might caused miracles to happen upon the earth.

Releasing the Word of the Lord

> Moses said to him, "Are you jealous for my sake? Oh, that all the people of the LORD were prophets, and that the LORD would put His Spirit upon them!"
>
> —NUMBERS 11:29

I believe we are living in a time when the Lord is answering the heart cry of Moses by anointing women with His Spirit to prophesy. All women are not prophets but all can move under unction of the Holy Spirit to operate in the gift of prophecy or the spirit of prophecy.

The right word spoken at the right time carries tremendous power. (See Job 6:25.) God has a word at the right time for every situation. I call this a word in season.

> The Lord GOD has given me the tongue of the learned, that I may know how to sustain him who is weary with a word; he awakens me morning by morning; he awakens my ear to listen as the learned.
>
> —ISAIAH 50:4

There is a right word in season for the weary. This is the tongue of the learned. Women who are learned in the prophetic can speak this word. Women who are learned in the ways of the Holy Spirit can speak this word. Women who have been instructed by God can speak this word. Our ears can be awakened to hear this word, and our tongues can be instructed to speak it.

Some people, based on their backgrounds, can get nervous when the conversation shifts to the prophetic. Some people think prophecy is emotionalism and something done only in charismatic or Pentecostal circles. Prophecy can really be seen from the wrong perspective, man's perspective. Prophecy is simply the revealed truth of who God is and His will for mankind. Prophecy can be further defined as speaking forth by divine inspiration the heart and mind of God to a particular people or certain situation. It is the dropping down of inspired speech into the hearts of men. Being God's creation, we need to know His heart for us. This is a valuable and vital element to our living well on the earth. We need to know God's heart and mind toward us.

The nature of prophecy has two dimensions: forth-telling and foretelling.

1. Forth-telling prophecy: This form of prophecy is in the realm of speaking forth—the prophet or believers speaking for God to the people, communicating the mind of God for the present.

2. Foretelling prophecy: This aspect of prophecy is in the form of prediction. The prophet speaks for God to the people, communicating His mind for the future. This level announces a new agenda on God's timetable for human history.

The authority and power of God are released through prophecy. Individuals, churches, and nations need to hear the word of the Lord. This is the key to the power and authority of women operating under the prophetic anointing as Deborah did. Modern-day Deborahs are spokeswomen of God. We carry the voice of the Lord to kings and nations. We will speak as oracles of God.

God's voice commands the armies in heaven and on earth. He is the Lord of armies. The army of God hears His voice and carries out His word. The word of the Lord will mobilize women from all walks of life to speak forth His words in due season.

For he is our God; and we are the people of his pasture, and the sheep of his hand. To day if ye will hear his voice…

—PSALM 95:7, KJV

Woman of God, we are the Lord's sheep, and we hear His voice. He leads us and guides us by His voice. This could be a still small voice, or it can be the word of prophecy. We need to hear His voice today, and we do this through the prophetic gifting ministered to us by prophets or prophetic believers or an impartation from the Lord Himself.

We need to be tuned in to what the Lord is speaking today. We need to know what He is saying to us in the present season. While God has not called all of us to the office of the prophet like Deborah, we can have a dimension of Deborah's anointing and grace to have our ears tuned to hear what the Lord is saying to His church today.

Prophecy will encourage you to move into the will of God. It releases faith to operate beyond what you are accustomed to. Deborah encouraged the leaders, rulers, and people of God to enter the battle and fight with the Lord. Prophecy breaks through demonic strongholds that are set up in the mind to hinder the plans and purposes for your life. The prophetic ministry, when delivered with accuracy and integrity, can restore the dignity and honor man lost in the garden.

For more detailed teaching and activation into the gift, spirit, or office of a prophet, please refer to my book *The Prophetic Advantage*.

Prayer to Activate the Gift of Prophecy

Lord, I believe that You are the Good Shepherd, and I am Your sheep. I believe Your Word that says I can hear and know Your voice. Your sheep know Your voice and follow You. I will not follow a stranger's voice. (See

John 10:4–5.) *Father, I humble myself as one of Your sheep and ask that You activate Your voice in my heart. I desire to hear Your voice on a greater level. Let the gift of prophecy be activated in my life. I desire to hear and release Your voice to my generation. By faith I stir up the gift of prophecy (2 Tim. 1:6). I rebuke all spirits of fear that will hinder the flow of the spirit in my life. Open my ears hear to hear Your voice. Awaken my ear morning by morning to Your gentle promptings. Give me the tongue of the learned that I might speak a word in season to those who are weary. (See Isaiah 50:4.) Lord, I open the doors of my heart that You may come in and teach me. I desire to dine with You. I desire that You will teach me Your ways. I desire that You will give me insight to things that are going on around me. I desire that You will give me the things I need to say for the task ahead of me.*

I declare that as I open my mouth, You will fill it with Your words! (See Psalm 81:10.)

I will prophesy to the dry bones in my generation.

I will prophesy life and hope to the hopeless. (See Ezekiel 37.)

Let my eyes be open to see from Your perspective. (See 1 Corinthians 2:9.)

Let my ears be open to hear Your truth.

Let my heart be pure to perceive Your will.

Lord, put Your eternal truth in my heart. (See Ecclesiastes 3:11.)

Chapter 7

DEBORAH AND BARAK

> Barak said to her, "If you will go with me, then I will go, but if you will not go with me, then I will not go." She said, "I will indeed go with you. However, the way you are going will gain you no glory, for the Lord will deliver Sisera into the hand of a woman." Then Deborah got up and went with Barak to Kedesh.
>
> —Judges 4:8–9

BARAK, A GREAT man of faith modeled and pioneered an example for modern-day ministry leaders to follow. His actions are a classic study in the wisdom of a man's acknowledgment of the potential power of a woman's contribution to a leadership team. Because of Deborah's undeniable connection to God and skillful leadership traits, Barak (as commander of Israel's armies) would not go into this battle without her, even when told that he would not get full honor for the victory (Judg. 4:9). His priority was the welfare of the nation. He knew that their combined efforts would ensure success as each brought their distinctive, God-given strengths to the challenge.

Deborah's quick and humble response is evidence that she also knew her presence was essential to the victory of the army of Israel. Contrary to popular teaching that Barak was a coward, I believe Barak was a man of faith who acknowledged the importance of the presence of God leading and directing him in battle. Deborah was a woman with a high degree of spiritual insight and character and was one of the few judges who was not corrupted by influence and success. Her presence on the battlefield inspired and incited the soldiers for war. Her presence gave them confidence that God was with them in victory.

Deborah replied to Barak that she would indeed go into battle with him. "However," she added, "the way you are going will gain you no glory, for the LORD will deliver Sisera into the hand of a woman" (Judg. 4:9). This was not a rebuke. Deborah wasn't even referring to herself but to the intent of God. Deborah was prophesying about the unique outcome of this battle. She was also referencing the fact that God has reserved certain victories for His women warriors.

Barak demonstrated honor for women in authority, and he was not afraid to share his success with her. He also was strategic and displayed the wisdom of God by having a woman anointed by God on his team. He didn't agree with the popular opinion of the day. He understood the power of the team.

I like how Matthew Henry's commentary describes their teamwork:

> See how the work and honour of this great action are divided between Deborah and Barak; she, as the head, *gives the word*, he, as the hand, *does the work*. Thus does God dispense his gifts variously.[1]

The team subdues their enemy under God's hand. Deborah and Barak are great examples of the power of collaboration.

Collaboration means to work with another person or group in order to achieve or do something. Collaboration is also the action of working with someone to produce or create something. If the body of Christ is going to meet its full potential, there must be new revelation and teaching regarding men and women working together in the kingdom. Some of us are afraid of the idea of working in collaboration with others because we feel threatened by it. "Will I get credit for my contribution?" we may wonder. And who wants to be one of many, just a spoke in the wheel?[2]

We must loose ourselves from that superstar mentality and embrace humility. "This narcissistic mind-set is endemic in our culture these days, fed by media (and reality TV)."[3] Sadly it's crept into the church. "Collaboration isn't about giving up your individuality. Quite the opposite: it's about realizing your potential."[4]

Barak realized Deborah's potential to lead in the midst of crisis, and he knew that was valuable to the team's success. Her prophetic gift to inspire and activate brought cohesiveness to the team. Before God informed Deborah of her role in His plan to rout out the Canaanites, she was already holding court and making civil judgments for the people in the hill country. They knew her to be a wise woman who had a connection to God. She was a prophetess and able to discern the mind and purpose of God.

In the time of the judges leadership may have been mostly bankrupt, but Deborah served because of her loyalty to God.

> [Collaboration is] about bringing your many gifts to
> the table and sharing them in pursuit of a common goal.
> It's about bringing your ideas, your passion, your mind,
> heart, and soul to your leadership and culture.[5]

As kingdom believers we must realize that we are all on the same kingdom team and are only as successful as what every joint supplies. God is requiring that men and women are "putting all and any baggage aside, bringing your best self to the table, and focusing on the common goal" of reaching the lost for Jesus.[6]

Effective Elements of Team Ministry

At the beginning of the universe God—the triune team—was functioning as a cooperative force. A male-female leadership team "should model the humility found within the Trinity, where we find both equality and submission among the Father, the Son, and the Holy Spirit. For church leadership, that means everyone must submit to Jesus and some form of human leadership as well. Nobody should wield absolute, unquestionable authority."[7] The Trinity is a team and our example of team ministry. Men and women are to submit to one another as to the Lord. Women and men are called to lead together, both exercising authority and dominion. A team can be defined as a group of people who are laboring together in unity in an organized way to accomplish a common objective toward God's purpose. Below you will find a list of effective elements of male-female leadership teams:

1. Honor

Honor can be defined as "respect that is given to someone who is admired, good reputation: good quality or character as judged by other people, high moral standards of behavior."[8] Barak honored Deborah's position in society. Deborah honored Barak's authority as commander of the army, and she allowed him to walk in his authority to gather the men for battle. Even though she received the command from God, she delegated the responsibility to Barak to gather the troops. Deborah humbly submitted to God's plan and wisdom over her own. This was not an example of a woman "doing the job because a man would not step up." Rather, it was a godly woman called by the Lord, sharing God's Word in the manner and order God had clearly outlined.

Barak honored Deborah's abilities and capabilities. Men must respect "women's education, experience and career obligations, instead of expecting them to fill traditionally female roles. If the CEO of a local bank loves making cupcakes for the Women's Banquet, fine, but it sure wouldn't hurt to ask her to chair the finance board....Male leaders should intentionally seek out female input. Women have an incredible wealth of wisdom, insight and parallel perspectives.... Be intentional about including women among your advisors." [9]

2. Purpose

Purpose can be defined as "the reason for which something exists or is done, made, used, etc.; an intended or desired result; end; aim; goal; determination; resoluteness; the subject in hand; the point at issue." [10] I like the last definition: "the point at issue." There are so many issues around women being used by God in ministry that we lose the point at issue, which is to destroy the works of darkness. It has been my experience that when people are hurting, they don't care if you're a man or woman. Deliverance from the oppressor is the main issue.

Deborah and Barak understood the purpose was to set a nation free. We must cultivate the same determination today; there must be a recalibration of purpose and true assessment of the heart and mind of the Lord as it relates to women in ministry.

3. Measure of rule

> But we will not boast beyond measure, but within the boundaries which God has appointed us, which reach even you. For we are not overextending ourselves as though we did not reach you, since we have come to you, preaching the gospel of Christ. We are not boasting of things beyond our measure in other men's labors. But we have hope that when your faith is increased, our region shall be greatly enlarged by you.
>
> —2 CORINTHIANS 10:13–15

A measure is the amount, length, breadth, height, or overall dimension of a thing.

In this passage of Scripture Apostle Paul is referring to your reach of authority. If we're going to work in an effective male-female team ministry, we must be careful not to go beyond the measure of rule and authority that God has given to each one of us. There should always be a set team leader. When you go beyond your set measure, you lack grace and authority, which could cause confusion and rebellion. No one has unlimited authority.

Deborah had prophetic insight and wisdom. Her revelation did not give her universal authority, and she respected Barak's military authority. She didn't usurp his authority to lead the charge into battle; she submitted and followed him.

We must remember that all members of the team are not gifted the same and do not operate with the same measure of faith. Deborah had incredible faith in God.

> She intends this as an appeal to Barak's own heart: "Has not God, by a secret whisper to thyself, given thee some insight of his purpose to make use of you as an instrument in his hands to save Israel? Hast not thou felt some impulse of this kind upon thy own spirit?" If so, the spirit of prophesy [sic] in Deborah confirms the spirit of a soldier in Barak: Go and draw towards Mount Tabor. She directs him what number of men to raise—10,000; and let him not fear that these will be too few, when God hath said he will by them save Israel.[11]

4. Diversity of gifts and administrations

Diversity of gifts and administrations make up the complexity of every team, but the key to unity is for every member to submit and align with the established order. Psalm 133:1–2 tells us "how good and how pleasant it is for brothers to dwell together in unity! It is like precious oil upon the head, that runs down on the beard—even Aaron's beard." Aaron was priest, which represents servanthood. We must learn to minister and serve the Lord by serving His people. The body of Christ requires a balance of male and female leadership to remain whole and healthy. To allow one half of the body to waste away while the other carries the weight (whether it's men or women doing the heavy lifting), results in a lopsided image of the church that is frightful to behold.

Prayer to Activate Unity and Collaboration

Lord, I thank You for the new thing You're doing in the body of Christ. I thank You for the unity and collaboration between men and women in ministry. Lord, I ask that You will cause the body of Christ to think outside the box of religion and tradition. I declare that walls of separation and division will crumble and fall. I bind every evil work of division and competition between men and women. I ask that You will pour out the bonding oil of unity. (See Psalm 133.) Let a new level of respect and honor arise between men and women. Let our conduct be worthy of the gospel. Let men and women stand together in one spirit and with one mind striving together for the sake of the gospel. (See Philippians 1:27.) Let us put aside our petty differences and humble ourselves under Your mighty hand. Lord, I pray that the body of Christ will move together in one accord. Let us be like-minded and walking in love. (See Philippians 2:2.) I repent for our self-ambitions and conceit. Lord, I pray that You will make us one as You and the Father are one. (See John 17.) Let us esteem one another better than ourselves. Let us identify each gift and not overstep our measure of rule. Let each person align in their proper rank and column as the army of the Lord. Let us collaborate and create to advance the kingdom of God in our spheres of influence.

Chapter 8

JAEL: A FIERCE WARRIOR

Most blessed of women is Jael, the wife of Heber the Kenite, most blessed of tent-dwelling women. He asked for water, she gave him milk. In a magnificent bowl she brought cream. Her hand on a tent peg, her right hand on a workman's hammer; she struck Sisera, she crushed his skull, she shattered and pierced his temple. Between her feet he sank, he fell, he lay; between her feet he sank, he fell; where he sank, there he fell, overpowered.

—JUDGES 5:24–27

"ARISE, SHINE, FOR your light has come, and the glory of the LORD has risen upon you" (Isa. 60:1). Yes, you! Arise from a place of inaction! Shine and become radiant with the purpose of the Lord. What are you going to do when God's spotlight of glory shines upon you? What are you going to do when the Lord brings right to your front door an opportunity to be used for His glory? Will you be prepared to step up to the challenge? Will you cower in fear? Will you falter between two opinions? Or will you step outside of every man-made religious box and seize the moment of opportunity to bring the Lord glory? That's exactly what our heroine Jael did.

When the national battle was brought to her front door, right into her domestic space, this Kenite woman stepped right up to the plate and staked her claim in history. Jael was a home-maker, a woman whom Deborah called blessed among women who dwell in tents. She is symbolic of a stay-at-home mom who proved to be valuable to winning the war in Israel. Jael was protecting Israel's heritage as the people of God. She knew the deeds of Sisera—his arrogance, brutality, and what he would do if she were a woman of a tribe he defeated. She would finish the battle Deborah had started and help to ensure forty years of peace in Israel. With Deborah she would bring *shalom* to God's people by obeying what she knew to be the will of God.

Jael is symbolic of an intercessor standing between God and the people. Her deed was an act of intercession. This is the hour that women must stand in the gap with prayer to save the next generation. There is a battle being brought to our front doors. We can no longer hide out in suburbia in our comfortable homes and pretend or be indifferent to the plight of many in our society. We must take action. Jael took action in order to save her family and possibly her people. Sisera had to be turned over to the Israelites. He became her sacrifice.

Jael reminds us that standing between God and the people can be a very dangerous place. Hard decisions must be made, and in the end there are times when we wonder if what we did was what God wanted. There is value to the women who stay home to raise the child and the women on the frontlines; they both get the same reward.

> Jael is linked with Shamgar, son of Anath, another fighter hero of early Israel (4:7; compare 3:31). And in the account of her slaying of Sisera, the poet calls for her to be blessed by women in tents (NRSV, "most blessed of women"; 5:24). Her deed is clearly heroic: she is a ferocious woman warrior, offering milk in a princely bowl, taking a tent pin and hammer in her hands, and crushing Sisera's head (5:25–27).[1]

The anointing on Jael dealt with the strongman and strongholds. She was positioned correctly to deliver a deadly blow to the enemy. She was in the right place at the right time using the right weapon. Jael was a stealthy heroine and a fierce warrior. She defied customary practices of hospitality in order to destroy the enemies of God. It was the call of God inside her that arose and broke through every limitation and man-made expectation to do something that had never been done.

> In those days everything connected with a tent was a woman's job, and the women became expert in all the phases of making, pitching, and striking tents. This is why Jael was able to turn her skill to good account, as with a tent pin in one hand and with a maul in the other, she drove the pin home through the skull of Sisera as he slept—a deed not allotted to divine leading although the victory over Sisera was.[2]

Jael represented a woman of boldness and accuracy. She hit the proverbial nail on the head. Many times when we obey the Lord, He is setting us up for the greatest breakthroughs of our lives. God is in the habit of anointing ordinary things and making them extraordinary. He took Moses's ordinary stick and caused it to be a conduit of power for miracles. He took Jael's skill with a tent pin and wounded the strongman. Not only did God proclaim that the seed of the woman would destroy Satan, He also said the way it would happen: the Messiah would "bruise" or crush the head of the serpent to destroy him (Gen. 3:15). This is exactly how Jael killed Sisera, by driving the tent nail through both of his temples, crushing his head.

Whether you are a woman on the frontline as Deborah was or a stay-at-home woman as Jael was, this is the hour we must let God take whatever is in our hands, i.e., skills, gifts, and talents, and let them be used for the glory of the kingdom.

Loose Yourself, Daughter of Zion

God is not only breaking women free from years of bondage and torment; He is also empowering them to set the captives free. Jael was one of God's secret weapons. Women are considered the weaker vessel, and the Lord used Jael as a prophetic type of how He has chosen the foolish things of the world to confound the wise (1 Cor. 1:27). Sisera was symbolic of a demonic strongman who set up strongholds that oppressed Israel for many years. Jael is a prophetic picture of a woman being empowered by the Spirit of God to take matters into her own hands! The Bible admonishes daughters of Zion to loose themselves. Zion is a prophetic word and symbol of the church.

> Shake yourself from the dust; arise, O captive Jerusalem. Loose yourself from the bonds of your neck, O captive daughter of Zion.
>
> —ISAIAH 52:2

The passage is a prophetic call for women to use our authority to shake ourselves free from bondage. God is causing women to be empowered to set themselves free so they can help other women be set free. This is the hour when the Lord is revealing Himself to women as the deliverer.

One of the major themes in the Bible is deliverance. Women have been crying out to God just as in the days of judges for freedom. The Book of Judges shows us God's mercy in delivering Israel from its enemies. God raised up deliverers to set His people free. The Lord in His mercy is sending deliverers to women. Deliverance ministry is simply anointing to bring victory and freedom to those in bondage. God is showing Himself strong on behalf of women.

When Jesus died on the cross, He became sin for us and destroyed the curse of the law, including the curse that caused men to rule women. It is only religion and deception that has caused women to be in bondage two thousand years later. Much of the church still has only applied His blood to men and has legalistically held women to the bondage of Eve's deception. The Bible makes it clear that Jesus came to destroy the works of the devil (1 John 3:8).

The Book of Judges points to the deliverance ministry of Jesus Christ. He came to preach deliverance to the captives. Women have been held captive by the deception of the devil for far too long. The hostile war proclaimed in Genesis 3:15 between Satan and women has been won through Jesus Christ our conquering King. This is the hour women will experience the full manifestation of Luke 4:18–19:

> The Spirit of the Lord is upon Me, because He has anointed Me to preach the gospel to the poor; He has sent Me to heal the broken-hearted, to preach deliverance to the captives and recovery of sight to the blind, to set at liberty those who are oppressed; to preach the acceptable year of the Lord.

Jesus came to preach good news to the poor.

Jesus came to preach the gospel to the poor. The poor represent the downtrodden, disadvantaged, and those held back from progress by people or circumstances. The Bible says in Hosea 4:6, "My people are destroyed for lack of knowledge." Many women have been held back simply because of lack of proper teaching and most of the time erroneous teachings. One major area of ignorance in the church is about gender equality.

Women are coheirs of God's grace. We are not second-class citizens in the kingdom of God. Jesus redeemed our position of authority and dominion. When men and women operate in unity, we create a true picture of God's glory in the earth. God has a redemptive plan for women. *Redemption* means to pay the fine for someone who has been in prison. The Lord Jesus Christ redeemed women from the curse and restored to us authority to rule with men. Jesus changed the status of women. We are no longer to be placed at man's feet but at his side.

Jesus came to heal the brokenhearted.

Jesus came to give personal attention to the brokenhearted by restoring them to emotional wholeness. This covers any and every human breakdown. The Lord is healing women from decades of bondage and oppression. These bondages have caused women to feel rejected by Father God.

The ultimate assignment against women is to get them to feel rejected by God the Father. The devil hates women. Satan has set up systematic methods where women have been rejected and treated as second-class citizens for centuries. Incorrect interpretation of Scripture has caused women to be rejected by the church and feel rejected by God. Women have been taught that they were created as subordinates to serve men. There is a growing number of women who are turning away from the church because it has marginalized them. Women want to be free to be the people God created them to be. Some have rejected Christianity altogether to follow New Age practices or other false religions.

I've been asked by many women in my ministry travels: "Why won't God do something about this? Why does God allow women to be so rejected by men in the church? If He is almighty, why won't He help us?" The bottom line always points to God. Through the actions of men Satan causes women to feel rejected or spurned by God. The good news is God is doing something! He has caused you to read the truth in this book and become a prophetic voice with a Deborah anointing to bring healing and truth to women.

Rejection can be defined as "the act of throwing away, the act of casting off or forsaking, refusal to accept or grant." [3] Some synonyms are *decline, refuse, repel, spurn,* and *disallowance*. Many times through male chauvinism God has been presented as one who rejects women. But Jesus came to release the spirit of adoption where we can cry out to God our Father. Jesus came to reveal the love of the Father to women.

The opposite of rejection is love. Love was the motivating factor that caused God to send His only begotten Son to the earth to redeem mankind and restore the relationship that was lost in the Garden of Eden.

Rejection causes a wound to self. When self is wounded, many abnormalities can, and usually do, develop within one's personality. The wounded personality is prone to become peculiar and unstable in behavior, attitudes, and opinions.[4] Also, physical infirmities often emerge out of the emotional stress of one's rejection.

Rejection, in the physical sense, is "an immune response in which foreign tissue (as of a skin graft or transplanted organ) is attacked by immune system components of the recipient organism."[5] Many times rejection can cause autoimmune diseases such as arthritis, thyroid disorders, fibromyalgia, lupus, allergies, asthma, type 1 diabetes, and more. These diseases are identified by how the body, due to some unknown trigger, begins to attack itself. This sounds a lot like self-rejection. God is healing women from self-rejection and low self-worth.

Jesus came to proclaim liberty to the captives.

Captives are prisoners. Jesus came to bring people out of the darkness of prisons and fortresses set up by people. This could be a natural and spiritual prison. There are many teachings that have caused women to develop demonic strongholds in the mind as it relates to their being able to minister in the church. Decades of ungodly beliefs must be broken before women can take their places of authority in the kingdom. This is the hour that Jesus is releasing women from restrictions imposed by people.

> Our belief system includes our beliefs, decisions, attitudes, agreements, judgments, expectations, vows and oaths. Any beliefs that agree with God (His Word, His nature, His character, etc.) are our godly beliefs. Any beliefs that do not agree with God (His Word, His nature, His character, etc.) contribute to our ungodly beliefs.[6]

Beliefs affect all of our perceptions, all of our decisions, and all of our actions. Ungodly beliefs set up strongholds in our minds that must be broken by the power of the Lord Jesus Christ. These are formed out of our experiences—hurts, traumas, and words people say.

Many times our ungodly beliefs combine with the demonic to produce a stronghold. This stronghold reinforces all of our ungodly beliefs. "A stronghold is an area of the mind where darkness reigns. It is a system of logic, rooted in a lie, that an individual has come to accept."[7] "Strongholds are incorrect thinking patterns that people develop over time, and are often set up and nurtured by demons through lies and deception."[8] Strongholds are fortresses set up in our minds. Jesus came to set the captives free. Paul tells us that the weapons of our warfare are not carnal but they are mighty through God to the pulling down of strongholds (2 Cor. 10:4). The Lord is releasing an anointing to cause all ungodly beliefs and strongholds that have held women captive to be destroyed.

The word *stronghold* comes from the Greek word *ochuroma*. It is used to describe a fortress, a castle, or a citadel. It also describes a prison with thick walls.[9] The devil has set up so many lies to stop women from moving in their God-given calls and destinies. He has tried to set up a fortress of lies designed to hold women as prisoners in captivity to his deception. The devil has tried to ingrain so deeply in our minds and belief systems that women are not called to places of authority. It has caused doubt, fear, and inaction. God in His mercy is eradicating by the power of the Holy Spirit every lie and illusion. No longer will women sit behind mental and emotional bars. God is unlocking every inner prison in our souls and making us whole.

The major way to be set free from ungodly beliefs and demonic strongholds is to be renewed in the spirit of your mind. "Behind every stronghold is a lie. Behind every lie is a fear. Behind every fear is an idol. Idols are established whenever we fail to trust in the provisions of God through Jesus Christ." [10] This includes His provision for liberty and freedom. We need to believe the truth of God's Word and make it the final authority in our lives. We are held accountable to the truth that we know. It is our responsibility to apply that truth to our lives. This is done by meditating on the Word of God daily to receive the truth of the Word. We must cast down every argument that exalts itself against the knowledge of Christ (2 Cor. 10:5). We must receive the mind of Christ (1 Cor. 2:16).

Jesus came to bring recovery of sight to the blind.

Jesus came to bring recovery of sight to the blind both naturally and spiritually. Women will have a tremendous amount of revelation and insight into the plans and purposes of the Lord for their lives. This is a season of recovery of sight. God will cause women to see themselves from His perspective.

Jesus is liberating women who are oppressed.

God is removing every cause of sorrow, and then He is doing the positive work of transformation. Jesus came to set at liberty those who are oppressed. One major spirit the enemy oppresses women with is the spirit of infirmity. This is the hour when the Lord is delivering women in the area of sickness and disease. The term for *liberty* used in Luke 4:19 means "release from bondage or imprisonment."[11] It is also the Hebrew word *derowr* which means swallow, reference a bird swift in flight.[12] It's time for women to soar swiftly into the call and destiny the Lord has purposed for them. *Derowr* is also the technical term for the release of slaves and property every fifty years. God is bringing liberty and freedom to women worldwide. Where women have been treated as slaves and property, Jesus is declaring your freedom. Jesus is your jubilee! It's time to fly! It time to soar on the wings of the Spirit into your destiny.

Jesus specifically addressed the demonic spirit of infirmity:

> He was teaching in one of the synagogues on the Sabbath. And there was a woman who had a spirit of infirmity for eighteen years and was bent over and could not straighten herself up. When Jesus saw her, He called her and said to her, "Woman, you are loosed from your infirmity." Then He laid His hands on her, and immediately she was made straight and glorified God.
>
> —LUKE 13:10–13

Infirmity can be defined as "the state of being infirm...especially an unsound and unhealthy state of body."[13] This spirit is an end-of-the-age strongman assigned to use sickness to keep women ineffective in ministry. Many times demons are behind sickness and diseases. This daughter of Abraham mentioned in Luke 13, whom Satan had bound, clearly suffered from a rigidly fused spine. Her illness was attributed to a demon called a spirit of infirmity.

God is releasing a healing and deliverance mantle on women to be healed and released from years of sickness and bondage. A part of Jesus's commission was to bring healing out of His compassion for the suffering. Matthew 4:23–24 is the first

New Testament record of Jesus healing physical afflictions and bringing deliverance to the demonically tormented:

> Jesus went throughout all Galilee teaching in their synagogues, preaching the gospel of the kingdom, and healing all kinds of sickness and all sorts of diseases among the people. His fame went throughout all Syria. And they brought to Him all sick people who were taken with various diseases and tormented with pain, those who were possessed with demons, those who had seizures, and those who had paralysis, and He healed them.

Jesus came to proclaim the acceptable year of the Lord.

This is the time of favor and freedom for women. The essence of Jesus's ministry is listed in Luke 4:18–19, and it applies to women *and* men. The acceptable year of the Lord is the year of Jubilee.

Prayers to See Yourself As God Sees You

One of the most devastating strongholds to have is an incorrect image in your mind of who God is and how He feels about you. God is love, and He loves us so much. We must learn to think on things that are true as Philippians 4:8 admonishes us. Let's pray that this will take root in our spirits.

> *Lord, I choose to meditate on things that are true. I loose myself from all falsehood. I believe the truth of Your Word. By the power of God I uproot every lie and deception planted in my mind. Holy Spirit, let the truth of Your Word arise in my heart.*
>
> *"How precious also are Your thoughts to me, O God! How great is the sum of them!" (Ps. 139:17). Lord, I believe Your thoughts toward me are great. I'm always*

on Your mind. I believe that Your thoughts toward me are good and not evil.

As Isaiah 62:5 says, I believe You rejoice over me as Your creation. I am made in Your image. I bring You glory when I do Your will in the earth.

Lord, I have felt like You've forgotten or rejected me as a woman. I believe You love me, and I receive Your love. I loose myself from father rejection. I am not forgotten, cast aside, or thrown away. I receive the spirit of adoption, and I cry Abba, Father. I repent of these thoughts. I believe my name is written on the palm of Your hand.

Lord, open my spiritual ears to hear the songs You are singing over me (Zeph. 3:17). I choose to rest in Your love. I will no longer strive to be accepted. Don't stop filling me with Your love.

Prayers to Pull Down Strongholds

Lord, I know that my warfare is not against flesh and blood, so I am not angry or upset with men. I know my enemy has been the devil. I will not resort to carnal, weak weapons of hatred and retaliation. I choose weapons that are mighty and empowered by You to pull down strongholds. I choose to apply the Word of God. I plead the blood of Jesus to my mind. I use the name of Jesus to demolish strongholds set up in my mind by erroneous teaching. I bind every arrogant and rebellious idea in my mind. I cast down lofty imaginations and pride in my mind. I submit my thought life to the words of Christ, "Blessed are the pure in heart for they shall see God" (Matt. 5:8). By the power of almighty God, I demolish every stronghold opposing the will of God for my life! In Jesus's name, amen.

Chapter 9

DEBORAH THE PRESERVER

By a prophet the LORD brought Israel up from Egypt, and by a prophet he was preserved.

—HOSEA 12:13

JUST AS GOD stirred up Deborah and Barak to preserve the legacy of the children of Israel, He is challenging us to awaken out of our slumber and complacency and arise to preserve the legacy of the church. The body of Christ is in a radical transition time due to the shaking that is happening all over the world. The acceleration and advancement of radical Islam throughout the earth, the new surge of power with ISIS, and the critical dangers many face on our city streets every single day will only be overcome on our knees. The freedom we have to worship the Lord Jesus Christ and teach the words of Holy Scripture is being challenged every day. Pastors are leaving the ministry due to burnout, moral failings, and suicide. Many believers are leaving the church because they have no passion, no purpose, and no power.

The church has been lulled to sleep, and in many cases is oblivious to the raging battle against its very existence. But we must awaken and return to the core identity as stated by Jesus in Mark 11:17, "My house shall be called a house of prayer for all nations." It is time to put on the whole armor of God and embrace the mantle of intercession to stand in the gap for the souls of our nations. Deborah sets an admirable example for us in that she saw the needs of her people and envisioned herself in their solution. Woman of God, it is time to intervene, intercede, and speak out! Your voice is needed; we are in a war. People are perishing. You are an important element in initiating the manifestation of the revival of the Holy Spirit on the earth!

The entire fifth chapter of the Book of Judges was a blow-by-blow account of the natural war Deborah and Barak had to fight. She led the battle from the position of a watchman. Her goal was the preservation of Israel. This motherly, protective nature was revealed through her counsel and prophetic insight and was the place she led from as she facilitated the restoration of village life in Israel. Hosea 12:13 reveals preservation as one of the major functions of a prophet. The word *preserve* is the Hebrew word *shamar* which means "to hedge about (as with thorns); guard; generally to protect, attend to...beware."[1] This word emphasizes the protective element of the prophet's mantle. Deborah was a prophet who guarded and watched over the hearts and minds of a nation.

Modern-day Deborahs will have to fight a spiritual war in order to preserve kingdom life. We will demonstrate our role as watchmen through prayer and intercession. Women preserve, carry, and birth life. The preservation aspect of women's nature is needed in our churches today. One major place of expression will be in the house of prayer. God will raise up a company of women who will build a divine wall of protection through prayers, intercession, and petitions on behalf of the next generation. God will develop in these women a breakthrough spirit, as we've seen in Deborah, that will tear down every obstacle and destroy every enemy of the soul of the church.

Developing a Breakthrough Spirit

He who breaks through has gone up before them; they will break through and pass the gate and go out by it.

Then their king will pass on before them, the LORD at
their head.

—MICAH 2:13

Deborah and Barak led the Israelites in what appeared to be an
impossible victory over the mighty army of the Canaanites. For
eighteen long years Canaanites held Israelites in the bondage of
slavery and brutal oppression. But God raised up Deborah and
Barak to break the back of the enemy and set the Israelites free
from oppression. Though the enemy mobilized a massive nine-
hundred-chariot army against Israel, the courageous woman
Deborah issued a strong call to action and assured the troops of
the Lord's victory. The enemy was routed by the power of God,
and a great victory had been achieved over what appeared to be a
superior force. (See Judges 4:14–16.)

I want to give a clarion call to every woman reading this
book: Don't let the present condition of our nation discourage
you. If you will arise like Deborah and take action and pray for
this generation, the Lord will answer your prayers with great
miracles. Heaven responds when people pray. Your prayers will
release the power and blessing of God. Be assured that the presence and power of the Lord is with everyone who arises on His
behalf. Your prayers will release a breaking through of the power
of God into the earth realm. If women will lift up their voices in
prayer, they will deliver this generation from the deception and
oppression of the enemy. Prayer causes the hand of God to break
through into the affairs of mankind.

Breakthrough can be defined as "a military movement or
advance all the way through and beyond an enemy's front-line
defense; an act or instance of removing or surpassing an obstruc-
tion or restriction; the overcoming of a stalemate; any significant
or sudden advance, development, achievement, or increase as a
result of scientific knowledge or diplomacy that removes a barrier to progress."[2]

The Lord will burst all the confinements and go before you when you pray, just as He did for Deborah and Barak. When we pray, God's power is released and made available to bring victory and breakthrough into even impossible situations. Breakthrough prayer invades the impossible, making all things possible through Christ Jesus.

Keys to cultivating breakthrough

1. Keep God first (2 Sam. 5:17–25).

2. Persevere with a specific purpose (Gen. 11:1–6).

3. Keep the devil under your feet (Ps. 91:13; Luke 10:19).

4. Keep the fallow ground of your heart broken (Hosea 10:12).

5. Be driven toward personal change (Gen. 32:24–30).

6. Consistently speak what you believe (2 Cor. 4:13).

7. Become disciplined in prayer, especially praying in tongues (1 Thess. 5:17; Jude 1:20–23).

Every assignment we are called to fulfill and every place that's been ordained by God for us to access requires a breakthrough spirit. There will always be a measure of opposition because of the ruler of this world. We must develop a maturity and strong ability to live with resistance and know that our capacity for breakthrough is in Jesus. He has already broken through and gone before us. We must be obedient to pray to release breakthrough in the lives of others.

Releasing God's Justice Through Prayer

Learn to do good; seek justice, relieve the oppressed; judge the fatherless, plead for the widow.

—ISAIAH 1:17

God is raising up Deborahs who will administrate the judgment and justice of God through our prayers and intercession. Jesus taught that justice would be established through intercessory prayer. Justice must be sought from the Lord. This type of prayer is used by speaking God's Word.

Justice is about God making wrong things right. Justice is not revenge. It's the Lord balancing the scale of justice and righteousness, which are the foundations of His throne. We are living in an hour when our world is sliding down a slippery slope of immorality. As Christians our only hope for true justice comes from the Lord.

> Many seek the ruler's favor, but justice for man comes from the Lord.
>
> —Proverbs 29:26, nkjv

Jesus is the ultimate social reformer. He was the first to connect justice (social reform and making wrong things right) to night and day prayer.

> Shall not God *avenge* ["bring about justice for," nas] His own elect and be patient with them, who *cry day and night* to Him? I tell you, He will *avenge* ["bring about justice to," nas] them *speedily.*
>
> —Luke 18:7–8, emphasis added

There are two sides to God's justice:

1. Judgment (punishment, vengeance) to the rebellious who resist God's justice

2. Salvation (deliverance, vindication) to the redeemed as He makes wrong things right for them[3]

Here are some examples of God's justice (judgment/salvation) that makes wrong things right:

1. Healing: God's judgment on sickness is seen in the manifestation of healing power

2. Revival: God's judgment on compromise is seen in reviving the church by the Spirit

3. Soul winning: God's judgment on the kingdom of darkness is seen when people get saved

4. End-time judgments: God's judgments against the evil governments and their actions

5. Righteous legislation: God's judgment on unrighteous legislation (abortion laws, etc.)

6. Unity (reconciliation): God's judgment on division in the family, society, and the church

7. Holiness: God's judgment on sin, anger, pornography, drugs, and rebellion, etc.[4]

This is the type of justice for which the intercessor stands in the gap and prays, petitions, or pleads on behalf of others. The intercessors must cry out for the justice of the Lord to be released in the land. Isaiah 58:2 gives us clear instruction on how to release the justice of the Lord in the land:

1. Seek God daily.

2. Delight to know His ways.

3. Do not forsake the ordinance of God.

4. Ask of Him the ordinances of justice.

5. Take delight in approaching God.

Effective, Fervent Prayer

Confess to one another therefore your faults (your slips, your false steps, your offenses, your sins) and pray [also] for one another, that you may be healed and restored [to a spiritual tone of mind and heart]. The earnest (heartfelt, continued) prayer of a righteous man makes tremendous power available [dynamic in its working].

—JAMES 5:16, AMP

I like how the *Ultimate Bible Dictionary* interprets and defines "effectual prayer." It states that "'the supplication of a righteous man availeth much in its working,' i.e., 'it moves the hand of Him who moves the world.'"[5] There is an effective way to pray and there is an ineffective way to prayer. When we are talking about effectiveness, we are talking about rules, patterns, and principles to prayer. The Word of God is clear about different kinds of prayers and how we are supposed to pray them. I am going to focus on petitions or supplications, prayer of agreement, and intercession.

> First of all, then, I admonish and urge that petitions, prayers, intercessions, and thanksgivings be offered on behalf of all men, for kings and all who are in positions of authority or high responsibility, that [outwardly] we may pass a quiet and undisturbed life [and inwardly] a peaceable one in all godliness and reverence and seriousness in every way. For such [praying] is good and right, and [it is] pleasing and acceptable to God our Savior, Who wishes all men to be saved and [increasingly] to perceive and recognize and discern and know precisely and correctly the [divine] Truth.
>
> —1 TIMOTHY 2:1–4, AMP

In this passage of Scripture Paul is providing young Timothy with instructions for the church. Paul points out the primary purpose and focus of the church. He states first and foremost that his priority and the essential key to a successful life is prayer. Then he gives the type of prayer—petition and intercession—and the target of prayer—kings and those in position of authority. He goes on to give him the result of the prayer, which is peace and preservation of life. There is no one or nothing void of the reach of prayer. God can change any situation, touch the heart of any government authority. Prayer is universal. Let's take a look now at the prayer of petition, or supplication.

Prayer of supplication

This type of prayer is a strong, intense, spiritual kind of prayer that brings specific results because of its specific nature. *Supplication* is the Greek word *deesis*, which is a request or a petition that involves begging; it's intensely seeking of God. This word describes the prayer of a need and the prayer of request. In his book *Seasons of Intercession* Frank Damazio states that there are three elements to supplication:

1. A plea for the return of the created order of life, which has apparently been hindered until now

2. A steadfast, continuous, and unceasing prayer indicating a tireless pursuit of a given goal

3. An intense spiritual struggle, which will result in far-reaching ramifications for the whole work of the kingdom of God [6]

Prayer of agreement

> Again I say to you, that if two of you agree on earth about anything they ask, it will be done for them by My Father who is in heaven.
>
> —MATTHEW 18:19

In the verse above the word *agree* is the Greek word *sumphoneo.* It comes from the word *sum,* meaning "'together,' and *phoneo,* meaning 'to sound.' *Sumphoneo* is to sound together, be in accord, be in harmony. The word 'symphony' comes from *sumphoneo.*" Essentially, the word means "to agree together in prayer that is concordant." [7]

This is powerful praying. The main ingredient is agreement. Jesus is telling us that if we join with another, in agreement, He will be with us. If Jesus is with us, then that means He is agreeing also.

The prayer must be in agreement with the Word of God, which is the will of God.

> So in effect He is also praying with you. This is a very strong prayer. Notice that it says *you*. It must be something that you all are in agreement on. If you are praying for a third party (interceding for them) they must be in agreement with you. A prayer can never override another's will. God gave us free will and He will never violate it.[8]

I believe one of the major assignments against women is division. Satan knows that if women come together in unity and begin to seek God for revival and justice, God will break through with what will destroy the works of darkness in the earth.

Prayer of intercession

> Intercession is prayer that pleads with God for your needs and the needs of others. But it is also much more than that. Intercession involves taking hold of God's will and refusing to let go until His will comes to pass. Intercession involves going between and stepping between someone and his enemy in battle.[9]

The Hebrew word for *intercession* is *pâga'*, which means "to meet, light upon, join…fall upon, to strike, touch."[10] So we can say intercession is the readiness of a solider to fall upon or attack the enemy at the command of his Lord, striking and cutting him down. Intercession is also to strike the mark with lightning.

> Intercession is warfare—the key to God's battle plan for our lives. But the battleground is not of this earth. The

Bible says, "We are not fighting against humans. We are fighting against forces and authorities and against rulers of darkness and spiritual powers in the heavens above" (Eph. 6:12).

Intercessory prayer takes place in this spiritual world where the battles for our own lives, our families, our friends and our nation are won or lost.... Through intercession, you can take the offensive in the spiritual battle, building up your community, your nation and your world. As you follow God's call to rise up and take your place in the spiritual battle, God promises to "heal their land" (2 Chron. 7:14, NASB).[11]

Interceding for our nations, cities, people groups, families, or generations always involves a deliberate choice. One of the greatest expressions of the love of God is to lay down your life and pray. It is time for the Deborahs who have a heart to preserve a generation to rise up, stand in the gap, and bring down heaven's mercy on the undeserving. We must never underestimate the power of united believers to bring healing to the nations. We live in a wounded, oppressed world. We need modern-day Deborahs to intercede with a breakthrough spirit to break the yoke of the oppressor.

Prayer for Revival and Spiritual Awakening to Preserve Legacy

For this section I want you to do something a little different. Below I have provided you with prayer points that align with the message of this chapter. Since you are being activated as a modern-day Deborah—a preserver, a watchman—I want you to take these prayer points and develop your own heartfelt prayer to the Lord to release His justice upon the earth. If you have a prayer journal, a study Bible, and a pen, or if you use an app of some kind on your smartphone or tablet, go get what you need now and develop your own prayer strategy for this need.

1. Ask God to pour out deep conviction of sin, spiritual brokenness, holy fear, and genuine repentance among His people and leaders (2 Cor. 7:10; Eph. 6:14–20).

2. Pray for God to pour out spiritual hunger and a genuine spirit of prayer (Phil. 2:13).

3. Pray for God to bring unity and deep love among the churches. Many churches need healing among the members and from competing with other churches (John 13:35). The church must become one voice.

4. Pray for God to fill His people with a passion to see people saved (Rom. 9:1–3). Until God's people intensely pray for the lost and aggressively win souls, revival will tarry. Pray also for the lost by name.

5. Pray to the Lord of the harvest that He will give His people a greater revelation of the Great Commission and a passion for missions and planting churches. We need God's paratroopers to be released (Matt. 9:37; 28:18–20; 2 Tim. 4:5; Acts 8:4–8).

6. Pray for God to purify motives for revival. Ask the Holy Spirit to pour out His mighty purifying flood (James 4:2–3).

7. Pray for a mighty move of salvation and conviction to touch our culture: entertainment, government, education, and media (1 Tim. 2:1–2; Rev. 11:15).

8. Pray for a modern-day Pentecost, that the church will move into the greater works or fullness of Jesus Christ's ministry (Joel 2; John 14:12–14; Acts 2:1–4; 4:29–30).

Chapter 10

DEBORAH THE VISIONARY

> Where there is no vision [no redemptive revelation of God],
> the people perish.
>
> —PROVERBS 29:18, AMP

THIS WAS THE first prophetic word spoken over my life:

> You are My handiwork created unto Christ Jesus for
> good works. Yes, says the Spirit of God, you are My
> workmanship. You're not in this world by chance.
> You're not in this decade by chance. You are not an acci-
> dent. You are not a second-class citizen in my kingdom.

This one word changed the entire paradigm of my life. I am a
living testimony to the fact that without redemptive revelation of
God mankind perishes.

Perish means "to slowly break apart by a natural process; to
disappear or be destroyed; to cease to exist."[1] In other words
a life without vision is a life that slowly breaks apart, marking
time in this world, never reaching full potential, and fading into
eternity.

Before these prophetic words were spoken over me, I lived
under a cloud of confusion and father rejection. I lived in fear,
always wondering if death was waiting around the corner for
me. My very first memories of life were centered on watching
my mother die from a rare blood disease. I know now that
this tragedy caused me to develop a fear of death. My mother
was twenty-two when she died, and I was only three. I never

envisioned myself living past my twenties. Many people who knew my mother would always say, "You're just like your mother!" I know that they were trying to bring me some comfort and consolation, but in the mind of a young child I processed those words as, "You're going to die young too!"

My father and mother never married, and actually he never claimed me as his own. There were always conversations and controversy about "Michelle and her father," which opened me up to a spirit of abandonment and father rejection. I felt as if I were a mistake.

The words spoken by those prophets were simple, "You're not in this world by chance," but they carried spirit and life. There was a force and anointing behind those words that broke the yoke of rejection and fear of dying from around my neck.

It is the Spirit who gives life; the flesh profits nothing. The words that Jesus speaks to you are spirit and they are life. One God-empowered word brought hope, light, deliverance, and freedom. This prophetic vision from God began to plug the hole in my soul. The prophetic vision or word is simply the heart of God revealed for the benefit of someone else. It is not our destiny; it is more like a street sign intended to help us reach and discovery our destinies. The word spoken to me began to plant a seed deep within me to discover the purpose for which I was born and what it meant to be the workmanship of the Lord.

A Vision Prepared Before Time

Ephesians 2:10 states, "For we are His workmanship, created in Christ Jesus for good works, which God prepared beforehand, so that we should walk in them."

> Workmanship, *poiema* (poy-ay-mah); Strong's #4161: From the verb *poieo*, "to make." (Compare "poem" and "poetry.") The word signifies that which is manufactured, a product, a design produced by an artisan. *Poiema*

emphasizes God as the Master Designer, the universe
as His creation (Rom. 1:20), and the redeemed believer
as His new creation (Eph. 2:10). Before conversion our
lives have no rhyme or reason. Conversion brings us
balance, symmetry, and order. We are God's poem, His
work of art.[2]

There are things God ordained before we were ever on the
earth. Regardless of the circumstances surrounding your entry
into the world, God had a vision for your life. You are a work
of art designed by God to accomplish good works in the earth.
Do you know what that means? It means you are the product of
God's vision—and God's vision of you is beautiful.

God has already decided who you could be and should be.
Not mankind. He ordained you to be a woman and filled you
with His purpose. You are the outcome of something God envisioned, and through Christ He has brought about, and continues
to bring about, changes in you according to His picture of who
He designed you to be.

Living for God involves discovering His picture or vision of
what our lives could and should be. With this perspective in
mind, we women must live from this grid: there will be people
who will try to discredit our voices or devalue our right to minister as female ministers of the gospel, but we must draw our lives
from the Lord and seek only to obey His commands. We were
created with His purposes in mind. Until we discover His purposes and live them out, there will always be holes in our souls.

Vision brings clarity and definition to life. Vision brings struc-
ture to chaos. Vision provides inspiration. Vision is like oxygen
to the lungs. Vision can be the reason you get out of bed every
morning. Vision drives you and compels you to reach just a little
bit further and press a little bit harder. Vision can keep you alive
and breathing when life and all of its disappointments knock you

unconscious. Vision is like a defibrillator that delivers an electronic shock to the heart of hope that keeps you walking by faith and not by sight.

Vision begins with a burden from God. Then it becomes something you imagine, a picture you see in your soul. Vision is also a thought, concept, or object formed by the imagination.

Deborah had a vision for legacy. Deborah sets an admirable example for us in that she saw needs and envisioned herself in their solution. She encountered God and changed history. I believe she lived from the vision placed in her while she was in her mother's womb. Deborah gathered leaders around this vision and gave them a mission and purpose to accomplish.

I can't imagine living in the times she lived in. Israel was weak, defenseless, and far from God. I can imagine that morale was low and hope was gone. But Deborah had hope and a vision from God, and out of this she summoned the strength to quiet the voices of doubt and timidity. She called the people to battle, leading them out of idolatry and restoring their dignity. Deborah didn't expect Barak to take greater risks than she would for the vision God had given her or make a greater sacrifice than she was willing to make. She went into battle with him.

Deborah communicated her vision for war as a solution to the problem of oppression that had to be addressed immediately.

1. A vision begins as a burden from the Lord. Deborah had a burden to see village life return to Israel. Deborah's passion was to see peace in Israel once again.

2. God used Deborah's position as judge to prepare her heart to lead the people into battle. Many times our circumstances position and prepare us to accomplish God's vision for our lives. I can imagine hearing the turmoil and desperation of men and women in bondage awakened compassion in her heart.

Compassion will cause you to move to action to set the captives free. Jesus was moved with compassion to heal the sick (Matt. 14:14). One of the major advantages that the Lord has given women is compassion.

Strong's #4697: To be moved with deep compassion or pity. The Greeks regarded the bowels (*splanchna*) as the place where strong and powerful emotions originated. The Hebrews regarded *splanchna* as the place where tender mercies and feelings of affection, compassion, sympathy, and pity originated. It is the direct motive for at least five of Jesus' miracles.[3]

Deborah's vision began in the heart of God. She was a prophet who understood God's counsel clearly because He revealed matters to her by visible means. Proverbs 29:18 shows that when a society lacks any revelation from God (divine insight), such a society heads in the direction of anarchy: "Where there is no vision, the people perish; but happy is he who keeps the teaching."

Deborah held to the vision God gave her, and it kept her through everything she experienced. She viewed God's vision for her and her people through eyes of faith. This faith kept her from sin, shielded her from the sorrow all around her, and empowered her to see things through to the end. Here are five guidelines we learn from Deborah on how to see God's vision manifest in difficult times:

1. Receive God's promise with childlike faith.

2. Make the best of bad situations.

3. Stand with integrity in trials and temptations.

4. Walk in humility before God and man.

5. See everything in life from God's perspective.

You must be a woman of prophetic vision who has a heart to receive and believe that God-given dreams are possibilities. The Bible shows the presence or the absence of vision will determine whether or not people become lethargic, or worse—"cast off restraint," oblivious to the law (1 Sam. 3:1; Prov. 29:18). The presence of vision creates hope and brings change when articulated with enthusiasm. (See Luke 24:23.) The prophet Habakkuk directs that "vision" is to be handled according to certain principles if people are to embrace it (Hab. 2:2). The vision must:

1. Be written: "Write the vision…"
2. Be clear: "Make it plain…"
3. Be motivating to those who read it: "…that he may run who reads it"

Further, know that vision

1. Must be received with patience: "wait for it"
2. Has an "appointed time"
3. Is often delayed: "it tarries"
4. *But* its fulfillment will be certain

What Is a Vision?

A vision is "a clear and precise mental portrait of a preferable future, imparted by God" to His people.[4]

> A vision is a dream, an ambition. To "envision" means to see ahead or conceive something your heart desires. A vision is a mental view or image of something good and worthwhile which is not yet actually present. To envision means to imagine, plan beforehand, or consider the possibilities. Vision is for you, not just leaders. Vision is all about the future, not the past and present![5]

There are three elements we must consider if you are going to see vision fulfilled:

1. We must understand that our vision comes from God; it not something we imagine or think of overnight. Vision begins in the heart of God. God places in everyone a sense of purpose that only He can satisfy and fulfill. (See Ecclesiastes 3:11.)

2. Your priorities and spiritual gifts will help you focus on your vision; your vision begins where you are now, so you must face and solve your problems, and then overcome all barriers to fulfill your dream.

3. True realization of a vision begins with goal setting. Goal setting is much more than simply saying you want something to happen.

   Unless you clearly define exactly what you want and understand why you want it in the first place, your odds of success are considerably reduced. By following the [concept of smart goal setting] you can set goals with confidence and enjoy the satisfaction that comes along with knowing you achieved what you set out to do.[6]

1. Set goals that motivate you.

When you set goals for yourself, it is important that they motivate you: this means making sure that they are important to you, and that there is value in achieving them....Set goals that relate to the high priorities in your life....Goal achievement requires commitment, so to maximize the likelihood of success.[7]

To make sure your goal is motivating, as Habakkuk advises, write down why it's valuable and important to you.

Ask yourself, "If I were to share my goal with others, what would I tell them to convince them it was a worth-while goal?" You can use this motivating value statement to help you if you start to doubt yourself or lose confidence in your ability to actually make the goal happen.[8]

Habakkuk instructs us to wait for the vision, it may tarry or you may have some setbacks but keep moving toward the vision because it will come to pass.

2. Set SMART Goals

When thinking of how to set goals, I often reference Dr. Edwin Locke's pioneering research on goal setting. Dr. Locke, an American psychologist, developed the Goal Setting Theory, which says that for goals to be powerful, they should be designed to be SMART.[9]

Set specific goals.

Your goal must be detailed and explicitly stated. They should give instruction and blueprints pointing you in the way of your God-given destiny. Deborah's goal was to return village life to Israel. Her instruction was to rally a general to war.

Set measurable goals.

Time frames should be placed on your goals. This is done so that you have tangible evidence of the goal being accomplished. Deborah set springtime as the time frame for when Israel was to engage in warfare and overtake their enemies.

Set attainable goals.

Your goals should be achievable. They should not be out of your reach or ability to achieve, though they should challenge you to bring your objectives to a successful end. Deborah challenged Barak to follow the instructions of the Lord to exercise his abilities as general to lead the people in war.

Set relevant goals.

Goals should be relevant to the direction God has ordained your life. Your goals should be meaningful and purposeful to the passions in your heart. They should connect to the intended objective at hand and motivate you to be focused and consistent.

Set time-specific goals.

Your goals must have a set time of completion. This breaks apathy and procrastination. Setting a time frame for achievement creates urgency. When something has urgency, it requires speed and action. The oppressing bondage the children of Israel faced under Jabin required Deborah and Barak to move with speed and perform decisive action to bring about victory and set the children of Israel free.

3. Set goals in writing.

> Then the LORD answered me: Write the vision, and make it plain on tablets, that he who reads it may run.
> —HABAKKUK 2:2

Writing down your goal takes it from the dream and good intention realm to the realm of the possible. When you write down your goals, they become mile markers on the path to fulfillment. They give you a sense of where you are and how far you have to go to obtain completion. Many times Jesus declared and overcame the temptations of the devil by a simple decree of "It is written." Meditating and praying over your goals will motivate you to prioritize your efforts. Writing down your goals will help alleviate distractions that pull you away from your set path.

4. Make an action plan.

A list of clearly defined steps when implemented can create momentum. Momentum can be defined as the impetus gained by a moving object. Once you make the first step toward your goal, there is a sense of accomplishment that compels you to keep moving forward. That momentum will give you the strength or force that will allow you to continue to grow stronger and faster and more accomplished as time passes.

Prayer to Activate Vision

I thank You, my Lord, that I am Your workmanship. You are the Potter, and I am the clay uniquely designed to bring You glory. I ask, dear God, that You will awaken vision inside me. I don't want to waste my life doing things You didn't design me to do. I have a responsibility to You, my Creator, to use my life for Your plans and purpose. So I ask, dear God, that You would cause me to perceive Your heart and mind for me. Lead me and guide me that I might be all You designed me to be. Order my steps; show me the way I should go. Help me to set goals that are realistic and aligned with Your purposes. In Jesus's name I pray, amen.

Prayer to Break the Spirit of Procrastination

Lord, Your Word says that faith without works is dead. I break all spirits of procrastination in my life. I will write the vision for my life. I will not hesitate and procrastinate any longer. Your Word says that without a vision Your people perish. I declare that I am a woman of vision. I have a unique purpose to fulfill in the earth. I will not let the devil steal my time and days. I break all spirits of slothfulness and apathy in the name of Jesus. Amen.

Chapter 11

ANOINTED WITH POWER, DESIGNED FOR INFLUENCE

God has spoken once, twice have I heard this: that power
belongs to God.

—PSALM 62:11

MEN HAVE FOUGHT wars for power. Governments have been
overthrown for power. Brothers have killed brothers for power.
Mothers have sold their babies and bodies for power. Real, life-
changing power, mind-sustaining power, eternal-life-promising
power—that power belongs only to God. God wants to become a
powerful reality to the hearts and minds of mankind. He doesn't
want to be just a nice idea or a faith that helps us hold on. He
wants to be the power in our lives that heals the sick and shows
the world that He is real and He is here.

Heaven is ready to invade the earth with undeniable power
as in the days of the Book of Acts. There is a sound as a mighty
rushing wind being heard in the spirit realm. It's the sound of the
Holy Spirit empowering women with the Deborah anointing to
be agents of His glory and power throughout the earth.

Most Christians have no clue about the power of God and live
in an earthly, carnal, intellectual Christianity, where all they have
is nice words about God. God is blowing a prophetic trumpet
that is waking an army of God-fearing, love-motivated, and
demon-chasing women. The word has gone out, and great compa-
nies of women are being equipped and activated to proclaim and

demonstrate the power of God. This is an hour to know God and experience His exploits in your life. God is full of love and compassion and wants to clothe you with His divine power, to overcome the powers of sin, sickness, and darkness in your life and in your sphere of influence. The power of God demonstrates to us that the words of the Bible are not just some factious fantasy written by overly zealous men. Our Christian faith is not some theory full of intellectual reasoning. God is real. God's not dead! He is alive.

We must return to the ancient path and esteem the power of God as the foundation for our faith. The Word of God states that the faith of all believers in the Lord Jesus Christ should not be founded in human reasoning, but on the power of God.

> My speech and my preaching was not with enticing words of man's wisdom, but in demonstration of the Spirit and of power, so that your faith should not stand in the wisdom of men, but in the power of God.
> —1 Corinthians 2:4–5

We can argue and speculate all our lives, but when the power of God touches and transforms us, words are no longer needed. God wants all of His children to know with every fiber of their beings that He is real, He cares, and He has a purpose tailor-made for them.

If we observe men and women today, we will notice that some rely solely on their natural abilities, trusting only in technology, philosophy, logic, and other branches of human intellect and understanding. Others opt for witchcraft or other ungodly supernatural powers. Many are hungry for power outside of God. Many fail to realize that their choices lead to idolatry, bondage, and great dissatisfaction. For this reason God is raising up a new generation with the audacity to leave the boat of compliancy and fear to be agents of God's power and do miracles in His name. This new generation wants more because God has placed that desire within them. Today's generation of Christians is bored with a powerless gospel. Many are leaving the church and are opting for a godless spirituality. Others are depending on humanism because they are not seeing God's power demonstrated in their churches or in the lives of believers they are connected to. This must change.

The Holy Ghost and Power

The Holy Ghost is a vital force with a power far beyond any imaginable human power. The Holy Spirit is filling and anointing women, so why would He tell them to be quiet?

> Your answer lies in the one and only source able to break this yoke: the anointing of God! The outpoured Holy Spirit through the good news of the gospel is for you in all its fullness! God created you in His image and ordained you to show forth that image.[1]

It is time for women to arise and shine. The bottom line of this outpouring isn't to win a theological argument over the role of women but to further the gospel mission of the local church. We must be focused on seeing people come to faith and grow into mature disciples, and as women, the Holy Spirit is anointing and equipping us to do our part. We will be anointed to do just as Jesus did:

> God anointed Jesus of Nazareth with the Holy Spirit and with power, who went about doing good and healing all who were oppressed by the devil, for God was with Him.
>
> —Acts 10:38

Power to Transform Lives

God is releasing His power through women so that they will make the lives of those in their spheres of influence utterly different than they were before. There will be many who will challenge your authority to preach or teach the gospel. They will use every scripture out of context to silence your voice, but there will be one undeniable, unstoppable, unkillable force moving through you that will silence all of the gainsayers: the power of God! It will be the calling card for women in this next move of the Spirit. The power of God will be like the American Express Black Card in the earth: without limit. The limitless displays of the power of God will gain the attention of kings and presidents. Miracles will open doors of opportunities to preach the gospel in unusual places.

The Holy Spirit will give you power to change, transform, or affect people, places, and events. You will see this power at work in you so mightily that just your presence will cause things to change without your needing to directly force them to happen. This is the influence the Holy Spirit will grant you as you allow Him to fill you.

Deborah had a tremendous amount of influence. *Influence* is "the capacity to have an effect on the character development, or behavior of someone or something, or the effect itself."[2] She demonstrates the "effective way women 'lead' in the body of Christ. Deborah's life was lived in such a way that she earned respect from everyone." (See Judges 4:4–5.) "Her influence led to a 'strengthening' of others (4:24a). She was a source of strength to all who came to her. The influence of this godly lady made a significant difference—all became better because Israel restored her faith in God's will!"[3]

The Lord wants to reach people of all nations and bring them to salvation. He is using women who will operate in resurrection power in places where the people have been oppressed. We will be a sign and wonder to our oppressors. (See Isaiah 8:18.) In many nations women are considered nonthreatening, so oftentimes the authorities are baffled by women preaching in power and authority, so they just leave them alone.

The Lord is empowering women with miraculous power to influence human hearts for the glory of God. He releases miracles to show that He is a loving God who acts on our behalf. Supernatural healing shows God's compassion causing many to turn to Him. In Luke 7:16 when Jesus raised the widow's son from the dead, the people said, "God has come to help his people" (NIV).

Power to Break Through Barriers

Deborah had the courage to break barriers. She did not allow anything to stand in the way of seeing God's vision for His people to come to fruition. Developing a breakthrough spirit is the key to overcoming barriers designed to stop you from fulfilling your God-given purpose. As women we must embrace the power and supernatural ability through Jesus to break through every obstacle. We must not be afraid to unleash our ambition for the Lord. "We have to think bigger before we can be bigger."[4] Rather than going for the big, scary things that truly excite us, too often we set our sights too low, aiming for only what we assess we have a solid chance at achieving.

We must break through all of the decades of negative opinions. We must not let the negatives invade, overwhelm, or hijack our emotions and thoughts; they force their way into our minds. When our negative thoughts and opinions are renewed by the Holy Spirit, our mind-sets are transformed from "the fearful negativism of a carnal mind to vibrant, positive thinking of the quickened spiritual mind."[5] Positive attitudes only come by intentional, deliberate invitation. We must aggressively grab every opportunity to fulfill our destinies in Christ.

Barrier-breaking will involve rocking the religious boats. Women are great at nurturing relationships but are often fearful about saying anything that might jeopardize them. However, when you withhold your opinion and tiptoe around sensitive issues, you limit your value. Don't let your fear of rocking the boat keep you from challenging your religious mind-set and the religion in others.[6]

> Taking actions that put you at risk of failure, criticism, rejection…can be scary and emotionally uncomfortable. Yet, you cannot take on bigger challenges, build your skillset (your confidence with it), or expand your leadership influence unless you're willing to take such risks.… While there's a fine line between stupidity and bravery, you have to be willing to walk that line at times if you want to seize new opportunities and lead a rewarding [life in the kingdom of God].[7]

Power to Enlarge Your Boundaries of Influence

> "*Sing*, O barren, you who did not bear a child. Break forth into singing and cry aloud, you who did not travail with child. For more are the children of the desolate than the children of the married wife," says the LORD. "*Enlarge* the place of your tent, and *let them stretch* out the curtains of your habitations; spare not, *lengthen* your cords, and *strengthen* your stakes. For *you shall* spread out to the right hand and to the left, and your descendants *shall* inherit the nations and make the desolate cities inhabited."
>
> —ISAIAH 54:1–3, EMPHASIS ADDED

I would like to look at the above verse as prophetic instructions to women who will embrace the Deborah anointing to be a women of power and influence.

1. Sing—The singing of a new song represents a new season. New songs in Scripture represent the breaking of an old cycle. Deborah and Barak marked a new season of peace by singing. Singing also represents changing your attitude, mind-set, and environment. Singing also represents entering into a blessing

by faith. For many years women have been told by society to be silent, you shouldn't speak, but the Lord has given women permission to sing or, in other words, to preach, minister, and be vocal for Him.

2. Enlarge—Bigness; to grow wide and large; to give great scope to. I believe the Lord is challenging women to think outside the walls of the church or denominational organizations as it relates to ministry opportunities.

3. Stretch—Extend; spread out. The opportunity has been utilized to the max. New opportunities are waiting. Potential for prosperity awaits us. We must stretch beyond the obstacles and barriers.

4. Lengthen—Look to the future. Let the eyes of faith look beyond the natural.

5. Strengthen—Firm up what you already have; seize every opportunity.

6. Think BIG—Women must not see themselves as small or insignificant. This is the hour to dream big with God and think outside of the box of our minds to achieve great things.

7. Let them—The unforced rhythms of grace, not soul force. We must allow God to move through our lives without forcing things to come into place. God releases us to fulfill our dreams and use our gifts. We must not usurp His authority.

8. Don't spare—Don't hold back, darken, or hinder. Do not allow opinions of men, controversy, or fear to cause you to withdraw.

9. Expand—Break through resistance. There is a grace being released to women that will allow us to spread

beyond the borders of traditional roles. Through the creativity of the Holy Spirit, we are being empowered and our roles are being redefined.

Power and Wisdom

Power and wisdom are excellent qualities to possess. When they act together in perfect harmony, what an irresistible influence they exert. If a woman has power but not the wisdom to direct it, the outcome can be disastrous. On the other hand, if she has wisdom without power to enforce her concepts, stagnation and complacency settle in.

Deborah was a woman of wisdom.

> People came to get her advice from distant places. She was recognized as one who possessed sound judgment and level thinking. She could offer counsel that guided the erring nation back toward faithful obedience. How did she gain this "wisdom" (Pr 1:7). Our modern society needs women like Deborah who will arise and call for people to restore their loyalties to God's directions![8]

The fear of the Lord is the beginning of wisdom, which was the key to Deborah's success—and to yours as well.

Power and Prophetic Preaching

> The Lord gives the word [of power]; the women who bear *and* publish [the news] are a great host.
>
> —PSALM 68:11, AMP

The word *host* in this passage comes from the Hebrew word *tsaba'*, meaning "an army, a company, host, battalion, throng; a division of soldiers."[9] There is a special division of women warriors that is being awakened, trained, and endued with power from on high to prophetically preach the Word of God.

Prophetic preaching is a supernatural level of preaching that has a number of qualities. It must be biblical truth, judged by the word of God. It is preaching by divine inspiration and revelation. Many times it's considered as "chasing a rabbit." God will reveal an issue (or rabbit) that the listeners are dealing with, and the prophetic preacher will chase it with words, concepts, and insight on how to solve it.

Revelation includes knowing things you otherwise would not know, seeing things that have yet to occur, and perceiving things without prior knowledge. It is the mind of God revealed so that mankind can exercise dominion over time, space, and matter.

Preaching combined with the nataph anointing

Nataph is a Hebrew word meaning "to drop down as water, to fall in drops; to flow, drip, ooze, distill, trickle; to cause words to flow. This verbs occurs 18 times and refers to the dripping or flowing of water, rain, honey, myrrh, sweet wine and words especially words in prophetic discourse. *Nataph* is here translated 'preach,' but actually means 'drop your word.' In Micah 2:6, 11, *nataph* is translated 'prophesy,' or, 'let your words flow.'" [10]

Prophetic preaching is God's way of dropping His word in your spirit, right on the spot. The words and illustrations are exactly what the Holy Spirit wants to say to the people present at the time. The prophetic preacher is directed to share certain truths and expressions in a certain way using divinely directed scripture and illustrations.

Power and Authority

> They were astonished at His teaching, for His word was with authority.... They were all amazed and said among themselves, "What a word this is! For with authority and power He commands the unclean spirits, and they come out."
>
> —Luke 4:32, 36

There were two things about Jesus that caught the attention of people: power and authority. Jesus is releasing women who walk in these dimensions. Just as in the days when Jesus walked the earth, the religious systems challenged Jesus to speak in the name of God. God is using women as a sign and wonder to this generation. He will anoint their teaching and preaching with power and authority that will cause men to be astonished. God is assigning women as His authorized representatives in the earth to do the business of the kingdom. Women who believe on the Lord Jesus Christ shall do the works that He did and greater.

It's going to be important to understand the difference between power and authority. Satan has power, but he does not have authority. Power does not scare Satan, but authority does because it is what Jesus used to stop his works in the earth. Authority will defeat power.

The Greek word for power is *exousia*:

> One of four power words (*dunamis, exousia, ischus,* and *kratos*), *exousia* means the authority or right to act, ability, privilege, capacity, delegated authority. Jesus had the *exousia* to forgive sin, heal sicknesses, and cast out devils. *Exousia* is the right to use *dunamis*, "might." Jesus gave His followers *exousia* to preach, teach, heal, and deliver (v. 15), and that authority has never been rescinded (John 14:12).[11]

Kings rule their kingdoms through authority; they conquer by power. One of the signs of authority is determined by what you exercise your authority over. Jesus's rebuking the winds and waves was exercising His authority as Creator. Jesus through the cross gave women the authority or right or privilege to go into the world and make disciples of all nations.

Power, or *dunamis*, means:

...energy, power, might, great force, great ability, strength. It is sometimes used to describe the powers of the world to come at work upon the Earth and divine power overcoming all resistance. (Compare "dynamic," "dynamite," and "dynamometer.") The *dunamis* in Jesus resulted in dramatic transformations. This is the norm for the Spirit filled and Spirit-led church.[12]

Power is a gift you receive. It is given to you. Power is not something that is earned. Authority comes through your relationship with God. It is a result of your time spent in the presence of God. Authority is the product of your time spent studying the Word and worshipping the true and living God. True authority comes when Jesus becomes the Lord of our lives not just the Savior.

Prayers for Preparing for Expansion

I break every limitation and barrier set up in my life by the devil.

I break all stagnation and deformity in my life.

I break all small-mindedness. I loose myself from the grasshopper mentality. I will think big and dream big.

I will break out on the left and the right. I will advance in my call and move forward in my destiny.

I decree enlargement in my life.

I decree enlargement to my ministry.

I decree enlargement and new territory to preach the gospel. There is no speech or language where my voice will not be heard. My mouth will be enlarged over my enemies (1 Sam. 2:1).

Enlarge my heart so I can run the way of Your commandments (Ps. 119:32).

Lord, deliver me from fear and a low opinion of myself.

Enlarge my steps so I can receive Your wealth and prosperity.

I receive deliverance and enlargement for my life and my children. (See Esther 4:14.)

Lord, increase me and my children more and more.

Think BIG

In the name of Jesus, I will think the thoughts of God. I will dream with God. No longer will I consider myself least and smallest because I am a woman. I can do all things through Christ who strengthens me. I loose myself from fear and settling for less than what I deserve.

In the name of Jesus, I break through every glass ceiling. I prophesy to the borders of my life: increase! I cast down every demonic imagination and argument against the knowledge of Christ. I will not be double-minded about my call! I will walk in the Deborah anointing. I am a conqueror through Jesus Christ.

Lord, Your Word says that as a man thinks in his heart, so is he (Prov. 23:7). Let me think on Your thoughts toward me. For Your thoughts are as numerous as the sand on the seashore.

No shrinking back; no drifting

I rebuke every spirit of withdrawal in the name of Jesus. I will not retreat from the purposes of the Lord. I will move forward in the plans of God. I decree that I will not accomplish my call in my own strength. It's not by might nor power but by the Spirit of the Lord that every mountain shall be removed from my life. I shout, "Grace, grace," to the mountain of prejudice, intimidation, and fear. God, give me Your heart for my assignment. Give me Your perspective that I might be Your mouthpiece in the earth. I will stand up against injustice. I am the righteousness of God, and I am bold as a lion. I am fearless *in the face of danger. I will preach the Word. I will go wherever You send me. In Jesus's name I pray. Amen.*

Occupy the position of FAITH!

I am a woman of faith. I stand on the promises of God. I believe the Word of God. I walk by faith and not by sight. I believe God to fulfill my destiny. I commit my ways unto Him, and He will perfect everything that concerns me. I receive the gift of faith. I believe that Jesus is the same yesterday, today, and forever. He is moving on my behalf. I am the righteousness of God through Christ Jesus. I, the just, live by faith.

Revelation knowledge

Let the spirit of wisdom and revelation rest upon my life. Lord, You are the God who reveal secrets; reveal Your secrets unto me (Amos 3:7). Let the eyes of my understanding be enlightened; let my heart be flooded with light. Open my eyes so that I might behold wondrous things from Your law. I rebuke spiritual blindness. Let me understand the mystery of Your kingdom. Let me receive and understand Your wisdom. I want to know Your thoughts and mind for my life.

Chapter 12

LAPPIDOTH: THE MAN WHO TAKES CARE OF THE WOMAN DEBORAH

> Now Deborah, the wife of Lappidoth, was a prophetess. She judges Israel at that time.
>
> —JUDGES 4:4

As WE HAVE discovered, Deborah was one of the most multi-talented women of the Bible—a wife, mother, prophetess, judge, poetess, singer, and political leader. Her life is a powerful example of the power that womanhood has to influence society for good. God gifted Deborah with the ability to cast vision, build teams, and develop strategies in order to deliver God's people. But at the end of the day who took care of the natural woman? How did she find peace and encouragement for her soul aside from her relationship with God?

Can you imagine listening and settling disputes all day long? How could she be so successful in balancing all the roles and responsibilities in society and still remain emotionally healthy? I believe the answer can be found in her relationship with her husband, Lappidoth. Now, I am not saying that in order for women to be strong leaders they have to have a husband. I believe that Lappidoth's love as a husband was one of the sources of Deborah's strength.

Our first introduction to Lappidoth is through his connection to his wife, Deborah. In my research of Lappidoth I found that all of history pointed to or referenced his function as Deborah's husband. To the natural eye it appears that Lappidoth's respect and honor came because of Deborah. Some may even conclude that his role was insignificant in the history of Israel. Could it be that Lord was giving us a type and shadow of the power of a godly husband?

The world expects a woman to support her husband in his dreams. I've even heard some say, "The woman is the background to the man's foreground." Whether you are a male or female in ministry, Lappidoth's support of his wife in ministry speaks volumes.

The name *Lappidoth* means "lighter of torches or fanning flames." He is a prophetic picture of a man of God married to strong, female leader who has the ability to fan the flames of her destiny. As Deborah's husband, Lappidoth empowered her to use her gifts, to fully develop into the woman God created her to be, and to fulfill whatever God called her to do. I have heard of the horror stories where a woman strong in leadership married a man who through jealousy and insecurities then put the flame of her ministry out. Whether male or female, the person you marry can either advance or hinder your ministry calling. Deborah, the wife of Lappidoth, was the wife of torches or the wife of flames. You can even say because of Lappidoth's encouragement, Deborah was a woman of flames because she was so ignited by the love and encouragement she received from her husband. His support and encouragement allowed her the liberty and freedom to fulfill the call of God on her life.

Lappidoth was a picture of a godly husband. It does not appear that he interfered with Deborah's call as prophetess and judge. I can't imagine that, while Deborah was in the heat of the battle, her husband was at home waiting for her to cook dinner. I believe that Lappidoth was right there with her supporting her efforts.

God gives specific instructions on how husbands are to fulfill their roles. Husbands should love their wives, sacrifice for them, listen to their concerns, take care of them, and be as sensitive to their needs and hurts as they are to the needs of their own bodies. A husband is called to lay down his life for his wife. This may be why we don't hear anything about Lappidoth; he laid down his life for Deborah. A husband is directed to sacrifice his own interests in order to enhance his wife's interests. He is to nourish and cherish his wife's growth to maturity.[1] Who couldn't submit to a man like this?

One of the major needs that is often missed in strong women is their need to be cherished by their husbands. Our gifts and talents are graces given to us by God. The anointing on our lives is bestowed to us by God. We long to be loved and valued for our contributions to the family. The woman was designed to receive love and affection from her husband. There may be one thousand people giving her accolades and applauses, but there is only one opinion she really values—her husband's opinion.

Dancing With the Stars

> When you dance, your purpose is not to get to a certain
> place on the floor. It's to enjoy each step along the way.
> —WAYNE DYER[2]

Marriage and ministry are like one of the choreographed dances featured on one of America's popular television shows *Dancing With the Stars*. The long hours, hard work, and practice it takes to produce a dance is such a work of art—the stepping on toes, falling down, and getting up and not forgetting the costume malfunctions. After the hard work the rewards are great. The dance partners are moving together in perfect harmony. The dance steps are synchronized to a beautiful song—the male dancer leading, and the female dancer following. The leading and following this dominant model stresses the mutual necessity and responsibilities as a complementary skill set. Both roles are indispensable to the unity and harmony of the dance. If both dance partners wanted to lead, can you imagine what a clumsy mess that would be? Men and women have different roles in partner dancing as well as in a marriage. There must be practice and hard work in the covenant of marriage. Each person must learn their God-given role and began to dance to the rhythm set in heaven.

Deborah was a woman of balance. She had accomplished all of these great feats for the kingdom of God, but she didn't neglect her role as Lappidoth's wife. They learned how to dance the dance of marriage and ministry. She learned how to balance her role as leader of the nation and still be Lappidoth's wife.

This description of wife is just as important and valuable as prophet or judge. Lappidoth's support of Deborah in ministry was not an abdication of his authority and headship as her husband. Deborah was a portrait of the virtuous wife. The key to her success was that she was a woman who reverently feared the Lord. Therefore, she wisely balanced her relationships and responsibilities. She also exemplified this truth spoken by Jesus, "Seek first the kingdom of God and His righteousness, and all these things shall be given to you" (Matt. 6:33). Taking a careful look at Deborah and her life will enable every woman to learn how to set her own priorities to manage her time, resources, roles and gifts that God has given her.[3]

Deborah was a woman of virtue: trustworthy, industrious, organized, and loving. Yet amazingly she was able to order the priorities of her personal world. Her husband totally trusted her; she submitted to her husband's leadership in the home and marriage. Scripture referred to her as a wife. A wife has the ability to fashion a good husband. She makes him feel loved and accepted, treating him with respect. She shows respect for his position of leadership. She does not undermine his authority. She offers encouragement, reflective interaction, and supportive interest.

Women with strong leadership gifts must be intentional about taking off the leadership hat and putting on the wife mantle. Just as Deborah understood her success in delivering God's people was in her role as mother in Israel, she also understood her role as the wife of Lappidoth. She knew what voice was needed in each occasion.

> Our attitudes toward our mate are governed by our attitudes toward God. A husband may fall short of a wife's expectations and of God's ideal for a husband. Nevertheless, the wife seeks in every possible way to be a good wife, using Christ as an example, who obeyed His Father and trusted in Him, even when His own people rejected Him (John 1:11).[4]

This will require vulnerability and submission. Yes, I said the V and S words: vulnerability and submission! I'll use myself as an example.

At the time of this writing I have been married for less than two years. I have been walking in the Deborah anointing for about fifteen years. I've traveled around the world as the "prophetess," giving wisdom and advice to leaders around the world. The prophetess gets invited to speak at conferences, where she is given the privilege of staying in beautiful hotels, on occasion ordering room service, mentoring sons and daughters, and in a nutshell giving orders and direction without rebuttal. God is now writing a new chapter in my life called "Michelle, the wife."

Once I met and married my husband, the prophetess mantle had to take a backseat to the new wife mantle. My lifestyle has changed as well as my responsibilities. I had to change in my attitude and actions. I couldn't interact with my husband as I would with one of my spiritual sons. I have to die to the role of prophetess so that something new and wonderful can be birthed. The Bible says in John 12:24 that a kernel of wheat must fall into the ground and die in order for it to produce much grain.

I am not saying that once you are married you can't minister.

I am saying that ministry has to look different and concessions have to be made for the success of the marriage. I had to let God give me His definition of what it means to be a wife. The concepts of being submissive and vulnerable and trusting a human being with the leadership of my life are things I must let the Holy Spirit teach me.

I have learned that God created both man and woman in His image (Gen. 1:26) with physical and emotional needs that only another human being can meet (Gen. 2:18). God clearly intended transparency and openness as part of His plan for the marriage relationship—vulnerability without shame (v. 25). God requires that the marriage partners are to "leave" their parents and "be joined" in order to become one (v. 24). They are to be willing to lay aside all that pertains to their old loyalties and lifestyles of separate goals and plans and be joined to one another. This "joining" refers to a strong, enduring bond—one unit bound together by unconditional commitment, love, and acceptance—resulting in a combined unit much stronger than either individual had been separately (Eccl. 4:9–12). Let me be clear about this: marriage was perfect in its establishment—one man and one woman in a lifetime commitment.

Prayer for a Godly Marriage

One of the major problems facing our society is broken families. Marriage is an institution God holds in high esteem, and He will judge the marriage-destroying spirit and will help you when you pray.

> *I cancel every assignment of darkness against my marriage.*

> *I bind any evil, seducing spirit trying to attack my husband, in Jesus name*

> *I pursue, overtake, and recover my marriage from the grips of marriage-destroying spirits.*

I rebuke every marriage-destroying spirit, in the name of Jesus.

I decree that what God had joined together no one will separate.

Let mutual love and respect flow in my marriage.

Let my husband lead our family according to the purposes of the Lord.

I release the gift of leadership upon his life. Let the wisdom of Solomon rest upon him.

I decree that my husband is a man of authority and he walks in the authority of the kingdom.

Let grace and love flow in our home. Let our home be a place where the glory of the Lord dwells. Let unity and oneness flow in our marriage covenant. I decree that my husband and I are one flesh. Therefore we are no longer two but one flesh. (See Matthew 19:6.)

Let us be tenderhearted toward each other. I rebuke the spirit of hardness of heart. I rebuke the spirit of divorce.

I rebuke every selfish spirit.

I rebuke the accuser of the brother and finger pointing. I decree that we will be quick to forgive each other.

NOTES

Introduction—Embracing the Call to Be a Woman of Power and Influence

1. Blueletterbible.org, s. v. *"quwm,"* https://www.blueletterbible.org/lang/Lexicon/Lexicon.cfm?strongs=H6965&t=KJV (accessed May 19, 2015).

Chapter 1—Times and Seasons of the Call

1. Dictionary.com, "fallow-ground," *Easton's 1897 Bible Dictionary*, http://dictionary.reference.com/browse/fallow-ground (accessed May 4, 2015).

Chapter 2—Deborah: The Judge and Deliverer

1. Blueletterbible.org, s. v. *"mishpat,"* "http://www.blueletterbible.org/lang/lexicon/lexicon.cfm?Strongs=H4941&t=NASB (accessed May 19, 2015).

Chapter 3—Deborah the Mother

1. Robert Hanley, "New Jersey Charges Woman, 18, With Killing Baby Born at Prom," *New York Times*, June 25, 1997, http://www.nytimes.com/1997/06/25/nyregion/new-jersey-charges-woman-18-with-killing-baby-born-at-prom.html (accessed May 5, 2015).

2. *Merriam-Webster's Collegiate Dictionary*, 11th edition (Springfield, MA: Merriam-Webster, Inc., 2003), s.v. "nurture."

3. Herbert Lockyer, *All the Divine Names and Titles in the Bible* (Grand Rapids, MI: Zondervan, 1988), 12–14.

4. Studylight.org, "Scofield's Reference Notes: Genesis 17," http://www.studylight.org/commentaries/srn/view.cgi?book=ge&chapter=017 (accessed May 19, 2015).

Chapter 4—Deborah the Worshipping Warrior

1. Jack Hayford, executive ed., *New Spirit-Filled Life Bible*, New International Version (Nashville: Thomas Nelson, 2014), s.v. *"shachah,"* 723.

2. Blueletterbible.org, s. v. *"proskyneō,"* http://www.blueletterbible
.org/lang/lexicon/lexicon.cfm?Strongs=G4352&t=KJV (accessed May 19,
2015).

3. Blueletterbible.org, s. v. *"yashab,"* http://www.blueletterbible.org
/lang/lexicon/lexicon.cfm?Strongs=H3427&t=KJV (accessed May 19,
2015).

4. Matthew Henry, *Matthew Henry's Commentary on the Whole Bible,*
s.v. "Judges 4," http://www.biblestudytools.com/commentaries/matthew
-henry-complete/judges/4.html (accessed May 21, 2015)

Chapter 5—Deborah the Honeybee

1. Elisabeth Elliot, *Let Me Be a Woman* (Carol Stream, IL: Tyndale
House Publishers, 1976).

2. Patrick Henry Reardon, "Judge Deborah," *Touchstone,* April 2000,
http://www.touchstonemag.com/archives/article.php?id=13-03-018-f
(accessed May 20, 2015); Rupert of Deutz, *In Librum Judicum* 6 (CCM
22.1158).

3. *TheWordDetective.WordPress.com* (blog), "The Honey Bee Prophetess (Part 1)," September 2, 2013, https://theworddetective.wordpress
.com/2013/09/02/the-honey-bee-prophetess-part-one/ (accessed May 20,
2015).

4. "The Name Dabar YHWH in the Bible," Abarim-Publications.com,
http://www.abarim-publications.com/Meaning/Deborah.html#.VUqz
645Viko (accessed May 20, 2015).

5. Ibid.

6. "Difference Between Honey Bees and Wasps," Orkin.com, http://
www.orkin.com/stinging-pests/bees/honey-bee-behavior/ (accessed May
20, 2015).

7. "The Name Dabar YHWH in the Bible," Abarim-Publications.com.

8. Ibid.

9. Jon Dyer, "Faith—Speaking Faith," JTDyer.com, http://jtdyer.com
/dailydevo/?p=246 (accessed May 20, 2015).

10. "What Does 'Busy as a Bee' Mean?" WiseGeek.com, http://www
.wisegeek.com/what-does-busy-as-a-bee-mean.htm (accessed May 20,
2015).

11. *New Spirit-Filled Life Bible,* New International Version, s.v. *"koach,"*
226.

12. Hannah Rose, *Straight From the Heart* (Bloomington, IN: Author House, 2013), 35.

13. This section adapted from Michelle McClain-Walters, *The Prophetic Advantage* (Lake Mary, FL: Charisma House, 2012).

14. Chabad.org, "Hayom Yom: Cheshvan 13," http://www.chabad .org/library/article_cdo/aid/5973/jewish/Hayom-Yom-Cheshvan-13.htm (accessed May 20, 2015).

15. Orthodox Wiki, s.v. "repentance," http://en.orthodoxwiki.org /Repentance (accessed May 21, 2015).

Chapter 6—Deborah the Prophetess

1. Portions of this chapter were adapted from McClain-Walters, *The Prophetic Advantage*.

2. Beginningandend.com, "The Prophetess Deborah—A Strong Woman of God," http://beginningandend.com/the-prophetess-deborah -a-strong-woman-of-god/ (accessed May 21, 2015).

Chapter 7—Deborah and Barak

1. Henry, *Matthew Henry's Commentary on the Whole Bible*, s.v. "Judges 4," emphasis added.

2. "Collaboration Is the Keystone to Leadership Success," Sarnia Lambton Chamber of Commerce, http://www.sarnialambtonchamber .com/Publications/First-Monday/Collaboration-is-the-keystone-of-leader ship-success.html (accessed May 21, 2015).

3. Ibid.

4. Ibid.

5. Ibid.

6. Ibid.

7. Jamie Munson, "10 Things to Remember When Building a Ministry Team," http://www.churchleaders.com/pastors/pastor-how-to /154149-10-things-to-remember-when-building-a-ministry-team.html (accessed May 21, 2015).

8. Merriam-Webster.com, s.v. "honor," http://www.merriam-webster .com/dictionary/honor (accessed May 21, 2015).

9. Jenny Rae Armstrong, "Why We Need More Women in Ministry," RelevantMagazine.com, March 8, 2013, http://www.relevantmagazine .com/god/church/why-we-need-more-women-ministry (accessed May 21, 2015).

10. Dictionary.com, s.v. "purpose," http://dictionary.reference.com /browse/purpose (accessed May 7, 2015).

11. Matthew Henry, *Commentary on the Whole Bible Volume II (Joshua to Esther)*, s.v. "Joshua 4," http://www.ccel.org/ccel/henry/mhc2 .Jud.v.html (accessed May 21, 2015).

Chapter 8—Jael: A Fierce Warrior

1. Tikva Frymer-Kensky, "Jael: Bible," Jewish Women's Archive, http://jwa.org/encyclopedia/article/jael-bible (accessed May 22, 2015).

2. Herbert Lockyer, "Jael: The Woman Who Killed a Man While He Slept," *All the Women in the Bible* (Grand Rapids, MI: Zondervan, 1988), https://www.biblegateway.com/resources/all-women-bible/Jael (accessed May 22, 2015).

3. Noah Webster, *An American Dictionary of the English Language* (New York: S. Converse, 1830), s.v. "rejection."

4. Tessie Herbst, *The Dark Side of Leadership* (Bloomington, IN: AuthorHouse, 2014), 322–323.

5. Merriam-Webster.com, s.v. "rejection," http://www.merriam -webster.com/dictionary/rejection (accessed May 26, 2015).

6. "What is a Belief System?", Restoring Your Life, http://restoring yourlife.org/resources/ungodly-beliefs-introduction.html (accessed May 26, 2015).

7. John Paul Jackson, *Unmasking the Jezebel Spirit* (N.p.: Streams Publishing, 2002), 173.

8. "The Ministry of Deliverance.... (We call it "Freedom Ministry"), Reclaimed Ministry, http://reclaimedministry.org/Freedom.html (accessed May 26, 2015).

9. "Fortresses in Your Brain," Last Harvest Fellowship, http://last harvestfellowship.com/bibleschool/fortresses-in-your-brain/ (accessed May 26, 2015).

10. Jack Hayford, *Acts: Kingdom Power* (Nashville, TN: Thomas Nelson, 2002), 103.

11. Strong's G859, s.v. "Luke 4:19," http://www.blueletterbible.org /lang/lexicon/lexicon.cfm?Strongs=G859&t=KJV (accessed May 26, 2015).

12. Strong's H1865, s.v. "liberty," http://www.blueletterbible.org/lang /lexicon/lexicon.cfm?Strongs=H1865&t=KJV (accessed May 26, 2015).

13. William White Whitney and Benjamin E. Smith ed., *The Century Dictionary and Cyclopedia* (New York: Century Co., 1911), s.v. "infirmity."

Chapter 9—Deborah the Preserver

1. James Strong, *Strong's Exhaustive Concordance of the Bible* (Peabody, MA: Hendrickson Publishers Inc., 2007).

2. Dictionary.com, s.v. "breakthrough," http://dictionary.reference.com/browse/breakthrough (accessed May 26, 2015).

3. Morgan Youngblood, "God's Justice in Response to Intercession," http://morganyoungblood.com/gods-justice-response-intercession/ (accessed May 26, 2015).

4. Ibid.

5. Matthew George Easton, *The Ultimate Bible Dictionary* (N.p.: Jazzybee Verlag, 2012), s.v. "effectual prayer."

6. Frank Damazio, *Seasons of Intercession* (Portland, OR: City Christian Publishing, 1998).

7. *New Spirit-Filled Life Bible*, New International Version, s.v. *"sumphoneo,"* 1247.

8. "How to Pray and Get Your Prayers Answered!", Revival Time Ministries, http://revivaltime.webs.com/apps/forums/topics/show/1600302 (accessed May 26, 2015).

9. "What Is Intercession?", CBN.com, http://www.cbn.com/spirituallife/cbnteachingsheets/keys-intercession.aspx (accessed May 26, 2015).

10. Studylight.org, s.v. *"pâga',"* http://www.studylight.org/lexicons/hebrew/hwview.cgi?n=06293 (accessed May 26, 2015).

11. "What Is Intercession?", CBN.com.

Chapter 10—Deborah the Visionary

1. Merriam-Webster.com, s.v. "perish," http://www.merriam-webster.com/dictionary/perish (accessed May 26, 2015).

2. Jack Hayford, executive ed., *New Spirit-Filled Life Bible*, New King James Version (Nashville: Thomas Nelson, 2013), s.v. *"poiema,"* 1647.

3. Jack Hayford, executive ed., *New Spirit-Filled Life Bible*, New Living Translation (Nashville: Thomas Nelson, 2013), s.v. *"splanchna,"* 1221.

4. George Barna, *Turning Vision Into Action*, (Ventura, CA: Regal Books, 1996), 35–36, as quoted in Leroy Bartel, "The Church's Vision for

Building People," EnrichmentJournal.ag.org, http://enrichmentjournal
.ag.org/200001/091_building_people.cfm (accessed May 26, 2015).

   5. Rodelio Mallari, "The Power of Biblical Vision," January 2012,
SermonCentral.com, http://www.sermoncentral.com/sermons/the
-power-of-biblical-vision-rodelio-mallari-sermon-on-miscellaneous-153052
.asp?Page=1 (accessed May 26, 2015).

   6. "The Golden Rule of Goal Setting," MindTools.com, http://www
.mindtools.com/pages/article/newHTE_90.htm (accessed May 11, 2015).

   7. Ibid.

   8. Ibid.

   9. SMART "Goals: What Are They? And Why Do We Set Them?"
TalentQuest.com, http://www.talentquest.com/corpsite/smart-goal
-setting (accessed May 26, 2015).

Chapter 11—Anointed With Power, Designed for Influence

   1. Bonnie and Mahesh Chavda, *The Hidden Power of a Woman* (Shippensburg, PA: Destiny Image Publishers, 2006), 21.

   2. Oxforddictionaries.com, s.v. "influence," http://www.oxford
dictionaries.com/us/definition/american_english/influence (accessed May
26, 2015).

   3. John L. Kachelman Jr., "Deborah: Israel's Holy Lady," Churchesof
Christ.net, http://www.churchesofchrist.net/authors/John_L
_Kachelman_Jr/people-ot/deborah.htm (accessed May 26, 2015).

   4. Margie Warrell, "Glass Ceiling or Glass Cage? Breaking Through
the Biggest Barrier Holding Women Back," Forbes.com, http://www
.forbes.com/sites/margiewarrell/2013/08/04/glass-ceiling-or-glass-cage
-breaking-through-the-biggest-barrier-holding-women-back/ accessed May
13, 2015).

   5. *New Spirit-Filled Life Bible*, New Living Translation, 1275.

   6. Warrell, "Glass Ceiling or Glass Cage? Breaking Through the Biggest Barrier Holding Women Back."

   7. Ibid.

   8. Kachelman, "Deborah: Israel's Holy Lady."

   9. *New Spirit-Filled Life Bible*, New Living Translation, s.v. "*tsaba*,"
682.

10. *New-Spirit Filled Life Bible*, New International Version, s.v. *"nataph,"* 1021.

11. *New-Spirit Filled Life Bible*, New Living Translation, s.v. *"exousia,"* 1256.

12. Ibid., s.v. *"dunamis,"* 1392.

Chapter 12—Lappidoth: The Man Who Takes Care of the Woman Deborah

1. *New Spirit-Filled Life Bible*, New Living Translation, 1542.

2. Brainyquote.com, "Wayne Dyer Quotes," http://www.brainyquote.com/quotes/quotes/w/waynedyer173500.html (accessed May 26, 2015).

3. "Woman of the Day Wednesday: The Virtuous Wife of Proverbs," July 31, 2013, Sisterhood School of Inspiration, http://sisterhoodschoolofinspiration.blogspot.com/2013/07/woman-of-day-wednesday-virtuous-wife-of.html (accessed May 26, 2015).

4. Pentecost Church of God Facebook page, "FRIENDS: A DIVINE ORDER IN FAMILY LIFE!!", January 19, 2014, https://www.facebook.com/permalink.php?id=111752726574&story_fbid=10152149714696575 (accessed May 26, 2015).

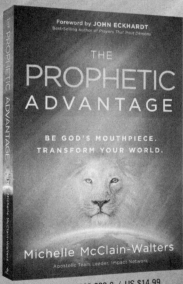

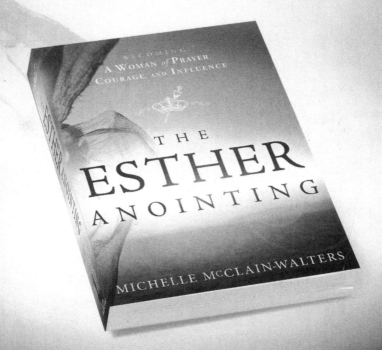